Blackstone's
Police Q&A

Crime

Blackstone's
Police Q&A
Crime

Second Edition

Huw Smart and John Watson

OXFORD
UNIVERSITY PRESS

OXFORD
UNIVERSITY PRESS

Great Clarendon Street, Oxford OX2 6DP

Oxford University Press is a department of the University of Oxford.
It furthers the University's objective of excellence in research, scholarship,
and education by publishing worldwide in

Oxford New York

Auckland Bangkok Buenos Aires Cape Town Chennai
Dar es Salaam Delhi Hong Kong Istanbul Karachi Kolkata
Kuala Lumpur Madrid Melbourne Mexico City Mumbai Nairobi
São Paulo Shanghai Taipei Tokyo Toronto

Oxford is a registered trade mark of Oxford University Press
in the UK and in certain other countries

Published in the United States
by Oxford University Press Inc., New York

A Blackstone Press Book

© Huw Smart and John Watson 2004

The moral rights of the author have been asserted

Database right Oxford University Press (maker)

All rights reserved. No part of this publication may be reproduced,
stored in a retrieval system, or transmitted, in any form or by any means,
without the prior permission in writing of Oxford University Press,
or as expressly permitted by law, or under terms agreed with the appropriate
reprographics rights organization. Enquiries concerning reproduction
outside the scope of the above should be sent to the Rights Department,
Oxford University Press, at the address above

You must not circulate this book in any other binding or cover
and you must impose the same condition on any acquirer

British Library Cataloguing in Publication Data

Data available

Library of Congress Cataloging in Publication Data

Data available

ISBN 0-19-926423-6

3 5 7 9 10 8 6 4 2

Typeset by SNP Best-set Typesetter Ltd., Hong Kong
Printed in Great Britain
on acid-free paper by
Ashford Colour Press Limited, Gosport, Hampshire

Contents

Introduction	vii
Acknowledgements	ix

1 State of Mind and Criminal Conduct — 1
Study preparation — 1
Questions — 1
Answers — 6

2 Incomplete Offences — 12
Study preparation — 12
Questions — 12
Answers — 17

3 General Defences — 23
Study preparation — 23
Questions — 23
Answers — 27

4 Homicide — 30
Study preparation — 30
Questions — 30
Answers — 33

5 Misuse of Drugs — 36
Study preparation — 36
Questions — 36
Answers — 41

6 Offences Arising out of Pregnancy and Childbirth — 47
Study preparation — 47
Questions — 47
Answers — 49

7 Offences Against the Person — 51
Study preparation — 51
Questions — 51
Answers — 56

8 Sexual Offences — 60
Study preparation — 60
Questions — 60
Answers — 66

9 Offences Against Children and Vulnerable Peopleb — 72
Study preparation — 72
Questions — 72
Answers — 76

10 Offences Amounting to Dishonesty, Deception and Fraud — 81
Study preparation — 81
Questions — 82
Answers — 90

11 Criminal Damage — 100
Study preparation — 100
Questions — 100
Answers — 104

12 Offences Against the Administration of Justice and Public Interest — 107
Study preparation — 107
Questions — 107
Answers — 110

Introduction

Before you get into the detail of this book, there are two myths about Multiple Choice Questions (MCQs) that we need to get out of the way right at the start:

1. that they are easy to answer
2. that they are easy to write.

Take one look at a professionally designed and properly developed exam paper such as those used by the Police Promotion Examinations Board or the National Board of Medical Examiners in the US and the first myth collapses straight away. Contrary to what some people believe, MCQs are not an easy solution for examiners and not a 'multiple-guess' soft option for examinees.

That is not to say that *all* MCQs are taxing, or even testing — in the psychometric sense. If MCQs are to have any real value at all, they need to be carefully designed and follow some agreed basic rules.

And this leads us to myth number 2.

It is widely assumed by many people and educational organisations that anyone with the knowledge of a subject can write MCQs. You need only look at how few MCQ writing courses are offered by training providers in the UK to see just how far this myth is believed. Similarly, you need only to have a go at a few badly designed MCQs to realise that it *is* a myth none the less. Writing bad MCQs is easy; writing good ones is no easier than answering them!

As with many things, the design of MCQs benefits considerably from time, training and experience. Many MCQ writers fall easily and often unwittingly into the trap of making their questions too hard, too easy or too obscure, or completely different from the type of question that you will eventually encounter in your own particular exam. Others seem to use the MCQ as a way to catch people out or to show how smart they, the authors, are (or think they are).

There are several purposes for which MCQs are very useful. The first is in producing a reliable, valid and fair test of knowledge and understanding across a wide range of subject matter. Another is an aid to study, preparation and revision for such examinations and tests. The differences in objective mean that there are slight differences in the rules that the MCQ writers follow. Whereas the design of fully validated MCQs is to be used in high stakes examinations which will effectively determine who passes and who fails have very strict guidelines as to construction, content and style, less stringent rules apply to MCQs that are being used for teaching and revision. For that reason, there may be types of MCQ that are appropriate in the latter setting which would not be used in the former. However, in developing the MCQs for this book, the authors have tried to follow the fundamental rules of MCQ design but they would not claim to have replicated the level of psychometric rigour that is — and has to be — adopted by the type of examining bodies referred to above.

These MCQs are designed to reinforce your knowledge and understanding, to highlight any gaps or weaknesses in that knowledge and understanding and to help focus your revision of the relevant topics.

I hope that we have achieved that aim.

Good luck!

Acknowledgements

As qualified police trainers, we have written this book to complement *Blackstone's Police Manuals* and to provide a source of improving knowledge of police-related legislation. It is important to recognise that full study of the relevant chapters in the *Police Manuals* is recommended before attempting the Questions and Answers.

Particular attention should be paid to the *Answers* sections and students should always ask themselves, 'Why did I get the question wrong?' and just as importantly, 'Why did I get the question right?'. Combining the information gained from self-questioning and the information contained in the *Answers* sections should lead to a greater understanding of the subject matter.

We wish to thank Alistair MacQueen and Heather Saward for their original vision and support for the project. Thanks also to Jane, Katie and Sarah at Oxford University Press for their continued support and patience.

Fraser Sampson remains, as ever, a source of encouragement to us both.

Huw would like to say a big thank you to Julie and their beautiful baby Hâf, for being there at all times, and for their patience and understanding during long evenings and weekends.

John would like to say thanks to Sue, David, Catherine and Andrew for their renewed support and encouragement when his patience was tested.

1 | State of Mind and Criminal Conduct

This chapter, which combines two chapters from the Blackstone's Manuals, tests what could be best described as the general principles of criminal law. When you consider that to prove its case, the prosecution must always prove 'the facts in issue' (see Chapter 10 in the *Evidence & Procedure Manual*) beyond a reasonable doubt, then knowledge of the *actus reus* and the *mens rea* becomes very important. In this chapter we will look at the general rule that an offence can be committed only where criminal conduct is accompanied by some element of fault and that both elements must coincide at the same moment in time. The precise fault element required depends upon the particular offence involved, as well as the fact that there is nevertheless a class of offences of 'strict liability', in which no fault element need be proved. In such cases, one can therefore have an *actus reus* without any corresponding *mens rea*. Also tested will be behaviours associated with criminal acts, both by one defendant and also other accessories. When answering questions in this chapter you should remember that, although they are based on substantive offences committed, they are testing the general principles of criminal law.

QUESTIONS

Question 1

LAWRENCE hates his wife and plans to kill her. He intends to cut her throat on Tuesday morning whilst she is still asleep. On Monday, LAWRENCE picks his wife up from work and is driving home; he is deep in thought about the following day's planned action. Owing to his inattentiveness, LAWRENCE drives through a red light, and his car is struck on his wife's side. She dies as a result of the accident.

2 State of Mind and Criminal Conduct

Could LAWRENCE be guilty of murder in these circumstances?
A Yes, as he has achieved his desired outcome.
B Yes, as he was thinking about the murder at the time of the accident.
C No, he cannot be guilty of murder in these circumstances.
D No, but he could be guilty of manslaughter.

Question 2

In law, some offences require a particular *mens rea*. Burglary, contrary to s. 9(1)(a) of the Theft Act 1968, is such an offence.

What is this type of crime known as? A crime of:
A Specific intent.
B Basic intent.
C Ulterior intent.
D Superior intent.

Question 3

In relation to 'negligence', which of the following statements is correct?
A Negligence is concerned with the defendant's standards.
B Negligence is concerned with the defendant's state of mind.
C Negligence is concerned with standards of a reasonable person.
D Negligence is concerned with standards of the law as laid down in statute.

Question 4

WHITE was broke and anxious to inherit his mother's money. One night he put potassium cyanide in his mother's bedtime drink with the intention of killing her. In due course, the following morning, it was discovered that his mother had died. WHITE was arrested on suspicion of murder. In fact, WHITE's mother had drunk very little; certainly, nowhere near enough to kill her. She had died of natural causes.

In relation to this, which of the following is true?
A WHITE is guilty of murder as there is a causal link between his actions and his mother's death.
B WHITE is not guilty of any offences as his mother died of natural causes.
C WHITE is guilty of attempted murder due to his intention.
D WHITE is guilty of attempted murder due to his actions, irrespective of his intentions.

Question 5

In relation to liability for an offence, which of the following statements is correct?

A A company could be held liable for an offence, but only if the offence is triable summarily.
B An employer cannot be prosecuted for offences committed by their employees, as offences are restricted to personal liability.
C A company cannot be prosecuted where an offence requires *mens rea*.
D A company can be prosecuted for an offence which involves strict liability, or where an offence requires *mens rea*.

Question 6

JENKINS was in a crowded pub and was larking about with her friends. She decided to throw a pint of beer over her friend BRYANT. Unfortunately the glass slipped out of her hand and smashed in BRYANT's face, causing cuts which required stitches.

In relation to assault occasioning actual bodily harm, what must be proved?
A Intention to commit any type of assault.
B Intention to cause the actually caused.
C Recklessness as to the assault itself.
D Recklessness as to the injury actually caused.

Question 7

HAINING has been charged with an offence of importing a Class A drug. He is pleading not guilty, stating that he only intended to import a Class B drug (an offence which carries a sentence of 14 years' imprisonment). However, when stopped by Customs and Excise Officers, it was found that the drugs he was importing were in fact Class A (which carries a maximum sentence of life imprisonment).

In relation to *mens rea*, has HAINING committed the offence charged?
A Yes, provided the prosecution prove he knew it was a Class A drug.
B Yes, it does not matter what class the drugs are.
C No, as he does not believe them to be Class A drugs.
D No, he could only be found guilty of importing Class B drugs.

4 State of Mind and Criminal Conduct

Question 8

ANDREWS was employed to operate a level crossing on a railway whilst a fault with the automated system was repaired. While at work, ANDREWS called his girlfriend on his mobile phone. He was so engrossed in the conversation that he forgot to close the crossing gates when a train was coming. A car was crossing at the time and the train hit it, killing the driver.

Is ANDREWS criminally liable in the death of the driver of the car?
A No, there was no positive action by ANDREWS to cause the accident.
B Yes, he had failed to carry out his duty and is criminally liable.
C No, ANDREWS did not have the relevant *mens rea*.
D Yes, as there is a causal link between his actions and their consequences.

Question 9

MILLAR intends to commit a burglary at a local electrical goods shop. He confides in NEWTON, who suggests he does it at 4 a.m. when it will be quieter, and suggests that MILLAR goes through a skylight into a room that is not alarmed. MILLAR thanks him for his advice and goes ahead with the burglary.

What is NEWTON's liability, if any, for the burglary?
A As a counsellor of the offence.
B As a procurer of the offence.
C As a principal offender of the offence.
D He is not liable at all for the offence.

Question 10

BALDWIN intends to murder his wife's lover by shooting him. He goes to see BOOKER, whom he knows to be an illegal gun supplier. BALDWIN tells BOOKER what he intends to do, and asks him to supply a gun. BOOKER is unconcerned whether the murder is successful or not, and is only interested in his profit from the deal. BALDWIN commits the murder, but is caught and tells the police about BOOKER.

Is BOOKER an accessory to the murder?
A No, he does not have the required *mens rea*.
B No, as he has no intention of aiding the actual shooting.
C Yes, he is reckless as to whether the shooting will happen or not.
D Yes, he is an accessory to the murder, as he knows the circumstances.

Question 11

JONES is a soldier living in the company barracks. JONES has a fight with STEYN during which he stabs him twice in the stomach with a bayonet. Realising the seriousness of STEYN's injuries, two other soldiers carry him to the nearby medical centre. STEYN is a large man and, due to his heavy weight, the soldiers drop him three times on way to the medical centre. On one of those occasions, STEYN hits his head very hard on the ground. On arrival at the centre, the overworked doctor fails to notice that STEYN's lung has collapsed and the treatment he receives from the doctor is less than adequate. STEYN dies from a culmination of all the injuries and the mistreatment he received.

Given the way STEYN was treated after his injury, is JONES criminally liable for STEYN's death?
A   Yes, the chain of causation is not broken.
B   No, due to the intervening act of the other soldiers.
C   No, due to the intervening act of the doctor.
D   Yes, provided the stab wound was the major cause of death.

Question 12

MURRAY is one of a gang of armed robbers who rob people in their own houses. They plan to go to GRAHAM's house and rob him. MURRAY is aware that knives will be carried, although he will not carry one himself. MURRAY is also aware that the knives may be used for violence, and that the rest of the gang is violent. During the robbery GRAHAM tries to fight back and is stabbed by one of the gang. GRAHAM dies as a result of his injuries.

In order to show that MURRAY is guilty of murder through joint enterprise, what would have to be proved?
A   MURRAY agreed to kill, using the knives.
B   MURRAY agreed to cause really serious injury using the knives.
C   MURRAY agreed to use knives for any purpose.
D   MURRAY contemplated that the knife could be used to cause serious bodily injury.

Question 13

JONES works for a major retail outlet. Whilst working on the video counter she sells a copy of 'Reservoir Dogs', which holds an '18' classification, to Stuart, who is 14 years old.

Given that the boy did not look 18, what is the retail outlet's responsibility with regard to the sale? (This is an offence contrary to s. 11 of the Video Recordings Act 1984.)

A No responsibility, only JONES will have committed the offence.
B No responsibility, unless the manager was aware of the sale.
C Full responsibility under corporate liability.
D Full responsibility under vicarious liability.

ANSWERS

Question 1

Answer C — Murder is a crime of specific intent, and requires a specific *mens rea*, i.e. an intention to kill or seriously injure. To be guilty of a criminal offence requiring *mens rea*, an accused must possess that *mens rea* when performing the act or omission in question, and it must relate to that particular act or omission. If, for example, a man accidentally kills his wife in a car crash on Monday, the fact that he was planning to cut her throat on Tuesday does not make him guilty of her murder (which makes answer A wrong), even if he was thinking about the planned murder at the time of the accident (making answer B incorrect), and even if he is subsequently delighted to find that his wife has died. Similarly, he could not be guilty of manslaughter (answer D) which also requires a specific *mens rea*.

Question 2

Answer C — Crimes of specific intent are only committed where the defendant is shown to have had a particular intention to bring about a specific consequence at the time of the criminal act. Thus, if burglary contrary to s. 9(1)(a) of the Theft Act 1968 was breaking a window with intention to enter only, then it would be an offence of specific intent (answer A). Basic intent requires no further proof of anything other than a basic intention to bring about a given circumstance, so if the s. 9(1)(a) offence was simply entering the building as a trespasser then it would be basic intent (answer B). However, as you must show not only intention to enter, but an intention to commit another unlawful act having entered, it *is* a crime of ulterior intent (answer C). Superior intent has been made up, which makes answer D incorrect.

Question 3

Answer C — Some would exclude negligence from a discussion of *mens rea* on the basis that *mens rea* is concerned with states of mind and negligence is not a state of mind (answer B is incorrect) but is rather a failure to comply with the standards of the reasonable person. Unlike strict liability, negligence still ascribes some notion of 'fault' or 'blame' to the defendant who must be shown to have acted in a way that runs contrary to the expectations of the reasonable person. A good example would be that of careless driving: in *Simpson* v *Peat* [1952] 2 QB 24, it was stated that if a driver was 'exercising the degree of care and attention which a reasonable prudent driver would exercise, he ought not to be convicted' of careless driving. It does not matter what the accused actually believes; it is what the reasonable person in the circumstances would have believed which counts (answer A is incorrect). Nor is it the standards laid down by law in statutes (answer D is incorrect).

Question 4

Answer C — There are two primary factors to any crime the *mens rea* and the *actus reus*. The mental element, or intention, is vital and there is a presumption that *mens rea* is required for a criminal offence unless parliament clearly indicates otherwise (*B (A minor)* v *DPP* [2000] 2 WLR 452). Therefore, answer D is incorrect. The relevant *mens rea* for attempted murder is intention to kill. WHITE has also taken action by poisoning the drink. However, where *actus reus* is proved, you must show a causal link between that and the relevant consequences. Despite his best efforts she had died, coincidentally, of natural causes. WHITE's conduct had not in any sense contributed to this and he is not guilty of murder (*R* v *White* [1910] 2 KB 124). Therefore, answer A is incorrect. Had he waited just one more day, there would be no criminal liability upon him. However, his intentions together with his actions make him guilty of attempted murder; therefore, answer B is incorrect.

Question 5

Answer D — This question addresses the issues of corporate liability. Companies have been successfully prosecuted for offences involving strict liability (*Alphacell Ltd* v *Woodward* [1972] AC 824) as well as offences which require *mens rea* (*Tesco Supermarkets Ltd* v *Nattrass* [1972] AC 153), making answer C incorrect. Liability is not limited to summary offences (making answer A incorrect), and companies can be liable for the actions of some of their employees under certain circumstances (making answer B incorrect).

8 State of Mind and Criminal Conduct

Question 6

Answer **C** — An assault or battery must be committed intentionally or recklessly, so the least you have to prove is recklessness, not necessarily actual intent (making answers A and B incorrect). If injury is caused, it need not even be proved that the injury was foreseeable. This is now clear from the decision of the House of Lords in *R v Savage* [1992] 1 AC 699, in which S aimed to throw the contents of a beer glass over B, but inadvertently allowed the glass to slip from her hand and break, with the result that B was injured by it. A conviction for an offence under s. 47 of the Offences Against the Person Act 1861 could be successful, because throwing beer over B was an intentional assault (indeed a battery) and that same assault had resulted in B's injury. Therefore recklessness as to the assault is all that is needed — not recklessness as to the extent of the harm likely to be caused (making answer D incorrect).

Question 7

Answer **B** — The *actus reus* is clear; he did import the drugs. We then have to consider the *mens rea*. The problem is that here there are two separate offences. If two separate offences have precisely the same *mens rea*, the problem disappears. Proof of the *mens rea* of one automatically involves proof of the *mens rea* of the other. This principle was applied in *R v Ellis* (1986) 84 Cr App R 235, in which it was held that an intention to import a prohibited substance is the *mens rea* sufficient both for importing a controlled drug of Class A and also for the separate offence of importing a controlled drug of Class B. Thus if an accused believed he was importing a Class B drug but was in fact importing a Class A drug, he can be convicted of the latter offence since he had the necessary *mens rea* of an intention to import a prohibited substance; answer D is therefore incorrect and there is no need to prove knowledge or suspected knowledge (making answers A and C incorrect).

Question 8

Answer **B** — Most offences require a positive act, together with the requisite state of mind for the offence to be complete. However, some offences are brought about by a failure to act and most of these arise from some sort of duty to act (this makes answers A and C incorrect). A person may in some cases incur criminal liability through failure to discharge his official duties or contractual obligations. A typical example is provided by *R v Pittwood* (1902) 19 TLR 37, in which P was employed to operate a level crossing on a railway but omitted to close the crossing gates when a train was signalled. P was convicted of gross negligence manslaughter. It is not a causal link which requires proof that the consequences would not have happened 'but for' the defendant's actions of omission; here, had the train been even one minute late, the accident would not have happened (answer D is also incorrect).

Question 9

Answer **A** — A principal offender must meet all the requirements of the particular offence, and for procurement there must be a causal link between his conduct and the offence. Counselling requires no causal link (*R* v *Calhaem* [1985] QB 808), all that is required is the principal offender's awareness of the counsellor's advice or encouragement — and this is true even if the principal would have committed the offence anyway (*Attorney-General* v *Able* [1984] QB 795). So he is guilty as a counsellor, not as a principal or procurer (making answers B, C and D incorrect).

Question 10

Answer **D** — One of the leading cases on the state of mind for accessories is *National Coal Board* v *Gamble* [1959] 1 QB 11, where Devlin J at p. 20 stated: '. . . aiding and abetting is a crime that requires proof of *mens rea*, that is to say, of intention to aid as well as of knowledge of the circumstances'. However, as Devlin J went on to point out, at p. 23, intention to aid does not require that the accused's purpose or motive must be that the principal offence should be committed:

> If one man deliberately sells to another a gun to be used for murdering a third, he may be indifferent about whether the third man lives or dies and interested only in the cash profit to be made out of the sale, but he can still be an aider and abettor. To hold otherwise would be to negative the rule that *mens rea* is a matter of intent only and does not depend on desire or motive.

There must also be an intention to aid the principal offender, and as such recklessness and negligence are not enough to convict an accessory. Thus, answers A, B and C are incorrect.

Question 11

Answer **A** — A defendant will not be regarded as having caused the consequence for which he stands accused if there was a new intervening act sufficient to break the chain of causation between his original action and the consequence in question — in this case the death of Steyn. The chain of causation can be broken only where the effect of the intervening act is so overwhelming that any initial injuries are relegated to the status of mere historical background. In the leading case of *R v Smith* [1959] 2 QB 35, which broadly follows the circumstances outlined in the question, the Courts-Martial Appeals Court held:

> If at the time of death the original wound is still an operating cause and a substantial cause, then the death can properly be said to be the result of the wound, albeit that some other cause of death is also operating. Only if it can be said that the original wounding is merely the setting in which another cause operates can it be said that the death did not result from the wound. Putting it another way, only if the second cause is so overwhelming as to make the original wound merely part of the history can it be said that the death does not flow from the wound.

It follows that a conviction could still be secured. Answers B, C and D are incorrect.

Question 12

Answer **D** — The main features that will determine MURRAY's liability as an accessory in a joint enterprise will be

- The nature and extent of the agreed offence
- Whether the accessory knew the principal had a knife
- Whether a different knife was used
- Whether the knife was used differently than agreed.

Proof of prior knowledge of the actual crime intended is not necessary if he contemplated the commission of one of a limited number of crimes by the principal, and intentionally assisted in their commission. For an accessory to be found guilty of murder as a joint enterprise it is not necessary for the prosecution to prove that the principal would kill; it is sufficient to prove that he might kill. The accessory, however, will not be guilty where the lethal act carried out by the principal is fundamentally different from the acts foreseen or intended by the accessory *R v Powell* [1999] 1 AC 1.

It is therefore enough that MURRAY contemplated that knives may be used, and used and that no actual agreement needs to be reached by the parties to the crime; therefore, answers A, B and C are incorrect.

Question 13

Answer **C** — This is an example of an occasion where the knowledge of certain employees will be extended to the company (answer A is incorrect). This was the circumstance in *Tesco Stores Ltd* v *Brent London Borough Council* [1993] 1 WLR 1037, where the Queen's Bench Division held that the knowledge that Jones had about the boy was also knowledge that placed a liability on the corporation. There is no need to prove any positive act by the company (making B incorrect), and it is not vicarious liability as this is mostly committed where a statutory duty has been breached, which is not the case in these circumstances (answer D is incorrect).

2 Incomplete Offences

STUDY PREPARATION

Having looked at the key building blocks of *mens rea* and *actus reus*, you now need to go on to consider specific criminal offences and their constituent parts. Before doing so, however, you need to get a few problematic situations out of the way.

The first of these deals with those occasions where the defendant, despite their best or worst endeavours, fails to do what they set out to do. These are 'incomplete' offences. The second area deals with defence to criminal charges — these are addressed in the next chapter.

When dealing with incomplete offences there are two key things to remember: first, that the physical impossibility of actually achieving what the defendant set out to do will not absolve them from criminal liability (and why should it?); and second, that some offences — such as summary offences and some incomplete offences themselves — cannot be attempted.

Finally, in this chapter we deal with the related area of police operations, where the evidential and substantive issues often overlap with those of the incomplete offences involved.

QUESTIONS

Question 1

In which, if any, of the following examples is the common law offence of incitement made out?
1. BROWN, who is 15 years old, encourages her teacher to have unlawful sexual intercourse with her but he does not.

2. FRAMPTON pressurises SMITH to encourage his brother to steal a car for FRAMPTON, however, SMITH's brother does not actually commit the offence.
A Both examples.
B Neither example.
C Example 1 only.
D Example 2 only.

Question 2

Officers intend to use a covert human intelligence source (CHIS) to further an ongoing operation. The CHIS will be used to attend a meeting of the target criminals which is being held in a public house, to record their conversations on tape and return the tapes to the officer in the case. In relation to surveillance, would this operation need to be authorised, beyond the authorisation of the CHIS?
A Yes, as this is directed surveillance.
B Yes, as this is intrusive surveillance.
C No, as the surveillance involves an authorised CHIS.
D No, as the surveillance is not in a private house.

Question 3

LANTZOS has been charged with an offence of statutory conspiracy under s. 1 of the Criminal Law Act 1977. He has been charged in respect of an agreement with others to commit a summary offence.

How, if at all, is this case likely to be dealt with?
A Withdrawn because you can only conspire to commit an *indictable* offence.
B Trial at magistrates' court only.
C Trial at Crown Court only.
D Trial at either magistrates' court or Crown Court.

Question 4

Jane and John RICE are married. They plan for John to defraud his insurance company over the reported theft of his car. They involve PEARD in their plan by asking him to hide John's car in his garage until the insurance company pay out. However, a few hours before the plan is initiated, PEARD said he did not want to be involved and the RICEs gave up the idea.

Who, if anyone, is guilty of conspiracy to defraud the insurance company?
A No one as the offence contemplated did not take place.
B No one as you cannot conspire with your spouse.
C Jane and John only.
D All three of them.

Question 5

In relation to the offence of conspiracy to defraud, which of the following situations would constitute an offence contrary to common law?
1. WATTS is a collector of model cars, and wishes to make a quick profit. He is aware that GRANT has a rare model Ford Sierra police vehicle, which is white in colour. WATT agrees with GRANT to paint the vehicle red and pass it off at auction as a rarer, more expensive Diplomatic Protection Group police vehicle.
2. TAYLOR is the licensee of the Masons Arms public house, which is wholly owned by a well-known major brewing company. He contacts his friend CROCKET who makes a very potent real ale home brew. They agree to install a barrel of the real ale and sell it at the pub, contrary to the licence TAYLOR holds which allows him to sell only the brewery's beers.

A Situation 1 only.
B Situation 2 only.
C Neither situation.
D Both situations.

Question 6

COLLINS is very keen to have sexual intercourse with HANSON. HANSON tells him she is only interested in his friendship and wants nothing more than that. One night COLLINS decides in his own mind that she will have sex with him if he forces the issue, so he hides outside her bedroom window. He forces the window open and enters intent on having sex, believing that she will allow it to happen. She is, however, not in the house.

In relation to an attempt to commit rape, which of the following is true?
A COLLINS commits the offence when he hides outside the bedroom window.
B COLLINS commits the offence when he enters through the bedroom window.
C COLLINS does not commit the offence, as recklessness to consent does not apply to criminal attempts.
D COLLINS does not commit the offence, as HANSON was not in the house.

Question 7

SHARMA has arranged with a burglar to act as a recipient of what he believes to be a stolen video recorder. SHARMA arranges for the video to be delivered to his house on Friday, and it duly arrives. A few hours later the police execute a warrant at his house and find the recorder. Despite extensive enquiries they cannot prove the video recorder was stolen.

Has SHARMA committed the offence of attempting to handle stolen goods?
A No, as he has received the goods he has committed the full offence.
B No, as the goods are not stolen he cannot be guilty of an attempt.
C Yes, he is guilty of attempting to handle the goods when he arranges to receive the goods.
D Yes, he is guilty of attempting to handle the goods when he actually receives the goods.

Question 8

In relation to an offence of vehicle interference contrary to s. 9 of the Criminal Attempts Act 1981, which of the following must the prosecution prove to make the offence complete?
A An intention to commit one of the further offences mentioned.
B An intention to commit any of the further offences mentioned.
C An interference only; no intention is needed.
D An interference along with evidence that the vehicle is a motor vehicle.

Question 9

YOUNG wishes to kill his wife who will not grant him a divorce, and looks for a contract killer. The police, however, are aware of his plan and send an undercover officer to meet him. YOUNG and the officer agree that for £2,000 the officer, posing as a contract killer, will shoot and kill YOUNG's wife. Naturally the officer has no intention of committing the murder.

In relation to conspiracy which of the following is true?
A As an agreement has been reached to carry out an offence, this is a statutory conspiracy.
B As an agreement has been reached to carry out an offence, this is a common law conspiracy.

16 Incomplete Offences

C As the officer will not carry out the murder, the offence of conspiracy is not made out.
D Although the officer will not carry out the murder, YOUNG is still guilty of conspiracy.

Question 10

Section 5 of the Regulation of Investigatory Powers Act 2000 allows for the Secretary of State to issue interception warrants.

For how long is such a warrant valid?
A One month.
B Two months.
C Threee months.
D Six months.

Question 11

In relation to the prevention of crime, what must the designated officer believe to authorise a covert human intelligence source (CHIS)?
A It is reasonable to prevent a crime.
B It is suspected that it will prevent a crime.
C It is reasonable in the circumstances to prevent a crime.
D It is necessary to prevent a crime.

Question 12

PRIESTLEY is employed by the National Crime Squad as a typist, in a support staff role. He goes home one evening and as a matter of conversation he tells his wife, a serving police officer, that he saw an interception warrant issued in relation to a local company, but does not mention which company it is.

In relation to unauthorised disclosures contrary to s. 19 of the Regulation of Investigatory Powers Act 2000, which of the following is true?
A PRIESTLEY cannot commit the offence as he is a member of the support staff.
B PRIESTLEY does not commit the offence as he does not name the company.
C PRIESTLEY commits the offence simply by mentioning it to his wife.
D PRIESTLEY commits the offence but has a defence that he did not disclose it outside the police service.

Question 13

Police strongly suspect that pupils from a local High School are dealing in class A drugs, and wish to use a juvenile Covert Human Intelligence Source (CHIS); however, the information is that the dealing is going on at the moment and it is urgent that the CHIS be authorised. Due to being unavailable it is not reasonably practicable to have the application for authorisation by the local Superintendent.

Which of the following statements is correct?

A In these circumstances an Inspector may give the relevant authorisation, and this can be oral.
B The relevant authorisation in this case will have to wait until the local Superintendent can give it.
C In these circumstances an Inspector may give the relevant authorisation, and this must be in writing.
D In these circumstances the Assistant Chief Constable can give the relevant authorisation.

Question 14

Police officer's wish to use directed surveillance on a newspaper office with a view to obtaining material that is of a journalistic nature, that will be used in the investigation of an offence of murder.

Who can grant authorisation for this directed surveillance?

A An officer of at least the rank of Superintendent only.
B An officer of at least the rank of Superintendent, or an Inspector in cases of urgency.
C The Chief Officer only.
D Any ACPO-ranking Police Officer.

ANSWERS

Question 1

Answer **B** — Although inciting someone includes pressurising or encouraging someone to commit an offence, and the other person need not actually commit the substantive offence, there are some exceptions. You cannot incite someone to commit

18 Incomplete Offences

an offence that exists for your own protection (e.g. unlawful sexual intercourse — *R v Tyrrell* [1894] 1 QB 710): thus, answers A and C are incorrect. You cannot incite another to aid, abet, counsel or procure an offence which is ultimately not committed (*R v Bodin* [1979] Crim LR 176), and therefore answer D is incorrect.

Question 2

Answer **C** — Generally, the action of covertly recording conversations will amount to some form of surveillance, which will be subject to authorisation. However, authorisation is not required where a CHIS is involved (s. 48(3) of the Regulation of Investigatory Powers Act 2000). So although the actions of covertly recording conversations in this way would amount to directed surveillance (answer D is incorrect) which would normally need to be authorised, here it does not need to be as a CHIS is involved (answer A is incorrect). Intrusive surveillance is broadly what it says it is, and is that which would intrude on someone's personal life. This would not include a public house and therefore answer B is incorrect.

Question 3

Answer **C** — A charge under this section can be brought for agreements to commit indictable or summary offences (answer A is incorrect). However, the offence is only triable on indictment (answers B and D are incorrect).

Question 4

Answer **D** — One of the exclusions to conspiracies is that husband and wife cannot conspire but this is when they agree together, as the sole conspirators. If, however, a husband and wife conspire with a third person who is not a child under 10 or the intended victim, all three may be liable to conviction (*R v Chrastny* [1991] 1 WLR 1381 confirmed in *R v Lovick* [1993] Crim LR 890), and therefore answers B and C are incorrect. Conspiracy does occur even though the offence intended never occurs and therefore answer A is incorrect. Once the agreement is made the offence is complete.

Question 5

Answer **D** — The common-law offence of conspiracy to defraud is expressly preserved by s. 5(2) of the Criminal Law Act 1977. It is defined in the leading case of *Scott v Metropolitan Police Commissioner* [1975] AC 819, where Viscount Dilhorne said:

... an agreement by two or more [persons] by dishonesty to deprive a person of something which is his or to which he is or would be or might be entitled [or] an agreement by two or more by dishonesty to injure some proprietary right of his suffices to constitute the offence ...

... it suffices if there is a dishonest agreement to expose the proposed victim to some form of economic risk or disadvantage to which he would not otherwise be exposed.

In the first situation there is clearly an agreement to charge the victim more than he or she should rightly have paid. The second situation deprives the company of its right to sell their own product (see *R v Cooke* [1986] AC 909 where buffet car staff were selling their own sandwiches on British Rail trains). Both options are correct and therefore answers A, B and C are incorrect.

Question 6

Answer **B** — In order to prove an attempted rape here you have to marry up the *mens rea* with the *actus reus*. The 'intended' or 'substantive' offence can still be 'attempted' even though it would be impossible and therefore answer D is incorrect. The mental element in attempted rape is the same as that required for the full offence; namely, an intent to have sexual intercourse coupled with, at least, awareness that the other may not be consenting (*R v Khan* [1990] 1 WLR 813). Therefore, answer C is incorrect. At what point then do COLLINS' actions become more than merely preparatory? In *R v Gullefer* [1990] 1 WLR 1063, the crucial issue was whether the accused had 'embarked upon the crime proper', but that it was not necessary that the accused should have reached a 'point of no return' in respect of the full offence. Being outside the window would be preparatory (answer A is incorrect). Entering would be more than merely preparatory as the offence could only be committed where the victim *is*, or in this case *isn't*!

Question 7

Answer **C** — This question examines the 'impossibility' rule as it relates to criminal attempts, and the courts have made it clear that an offence can be committed even though it was impossible (*R v Shivpuri* [1987] AC 1), as here where the goods are not stolen (answer B is incorrect). In *Shivpuri*, S was charged with an attempt to commit an offence under s. 3(1) of the Misuse of Drugs Act 1971. He confessed to acting as a recipient and distributor of what he assumed to be an illegally imported drug. It transpired (to his surprise) that the substance was not a drug at all but he was still guilty of an attempt to commit the s. 3(1) offence. So SHARMA would be guilty when he *agrees* to receive the goods, an act more than merely preparatory to the substantive offence, i.e. you do not have to wait until he actually receives them (answer D is incorrect). Having received the goods, which are not stolen, he cannot commit a handling offence, as that requires proof that the goods were stolen; therefore, answer A is incorrect.

Question 8

Answer **B** — This is a crime of specific intent, so you need to prove interference with a motor vehicle *or* trailer and as such answer D is incorrect (note there is no definition of what interference is). You do, however, have to show an intention to commit theft of the vehicle/trailer, *or* theft from it *or* TADA (taking and driving away); therefore, C is incorrect. It is not necessary to show intention to commit any particular one of the further offences, and intention to commit any of them would suffice; therefore, answer A is incorrect.

Question 9

Answer **C** — A person cannot be guilty of conspiracy if the only other party to the supposed agreement intends to frustrate or sabotage it. As the officer clearly will frustrate the agreement, answers A and D are incorrect. This was considered by the House of Lords in *Yip Chieu-Chung* v *The Queen* [1995] 1 AC 111, where N, the appellant's only fellow conspirator in a plan to smuggle heroin out of Hong Kong, was an undercover agent working with the knowledge of the authorities. The House of Lords held that, if N's purpose had been to prevent the heroin being smuggled, no indictable conspiracy would have existed. Their Lordships said:

> The crime of conspiracy requires an agreement between two or more persons to commit an unlawful act with the intention of carrying it out. It is the intention to carry out the crime that constitutes the necessary *mens rea* for the offence. . . . [A]n undercover agent who has no intention of committing the crime lacks the necessary *mens rea* to be a conspirator.

Conspiracy requires an agreement which will amount to or involve the commission of an offence. Where no such offence is likely, the offence is not made out. Common law conspiracy involves conspiracy to defraud only and therefore B is incorrect.

Question 10

Answer **C** — An interception warrant is normally valid for three months but can be renewed on certain grounds (answers A, B and D are incorrect).

Question 11

Answer **D** — A designated person must not authorise any activity by a CHIS unless he or she believes it is necessary, and that to do so is proportionate to what is being sought. It is not enough to believe it was reasonable (answer A is incorrect), nor that it is reasonable in the circumstances (answer C is incorrect), nor that it was suspected (answer B is incorrect). It can only be authorised if the designated officer believes that it is both necessary and proportionate to the legitimate objective of the operation.

Question 12

Answer **C** — This offence applies to police officers and support staff alike, and would apply to anyone involved in an investigation (answer A is incorrect). It deals with interception warrants and requires those to whom it applies, to keep secret any knowledge they have in relation to that warrant. The offence would be committed by simply mentioning the warrant's existence, irrespective of whether any individual or company was named (answer B is incorrect). Although there is a defence, it relates to the accused taking steps to prevent the disclosure, in the circumstances of the question this is clearly not the case and PRIESTLEY has no defence (answer D is incorrect). Note that there are other defences available to s. 19, but they relate to communication with legal advisors and the Interception of Communications Commissioner.

Question 13

Answer **D** — The people who can give authorisations for a CHIS are prescribed by s. 30 Regulation of Investigatory Powers Act 2000, and in the case of police services in England and Wales the relevant rank is Superintendent and above, not necessarily the local Superintendent; therefore, Answer B is incorrect. However, where it is not reasonably practicable to have the application for authorisation considered by someone of that rank, and having regard to the urgency of that case, an Inspector may, in general, give the relevant authorisation. As with other parts of the Act, the Codes of Practice do constrain this power, and where the CHIS is a juvenile of likely to obtain confidential material the code does not allow an Inspector to give the relevant authority, orally or in writing therefore answers B and C are incorrect.

Question 14

Answer C — In general, directed surveillance can be authorised by an officer of at least the rank of Superintendent, or an Inspector in cases of urgency, making answer A incorrect. However, the Codes of Practice again restrict this practice. For instance, where the material sought by the surveillance is subject to legal privilege, or is confidential personal information of journalistic material, the only person who can authorise it is the Chief Officer; therefore, answer B and D incorrect.

3 General Defences

STUDY PREPARATION

There is little point in collecting evidence, arresting and charging a person only to find that they raise a specific or general defence at trial — a defence which the investigating officer could have addressed in interview or when taking witness statements. For this reason alone it is important to know what defences may exist in relation to certain offences. Similarly, as the police are under a duty to investigate fully and impartially it is important to know what defences may be available to a defendant.

A number of offences have specific defences contained in the relevant statute, and these are (not surprisingly) called statutory defences. In addition, there are a number of 'general defences' some of which are statutory and others existing at common law. It is and helpful to divide general defences into two categories:

1. Those which involve a denial of the basic requirements of *mens rea* and voluntary conduct (the defences of mistake and automatism are best regarded in this way).
2. Those which do not deny these basic requirements but which rely on other circumstances of excuse or justification, as in the defences of duress and self-defence.

The integration of the Human Rights Act 1998 and the European Convention on Human Rights into English law is also important in this area of study.

QUESTIONS

Question 1

SMITH is driving his motor vehicle at 70 mph in the outside lane of a motorway, with his window open. A bee flies in through the window and as he fears being stung,

SMITH tries to kill it with his newspaper. Momentarily distracted, he fails to notice the vehicle in front has slowed and he runs into the back of it. Police investigate and he is reported for an offence of careless driving.

In these circumstances could SMITH use the defence of automatism?

A Yes, his actions were not voluntary or willed.
B Yes, as he cannot be held liable for his actions as he lost control.
C No, although a reflex action it would not amount to automatism.
D Yes, provided he could not have foreseen the bee flying in.

Question 2

HERBERT has been arguing over several months with his neighbour, HUGHES, about a shared driveway, and is now at his wits' end. HERBERT decides it is time for action and intends to assault HUGHES to teach him a lesson. Armed with a baseball bat, HERBERT waits for HUGHES to return from work. To aid his courage he drinks half a bottle of scotch, and is intoxicated when HUGHES arrives home. HERBERT runs out and strikes HUGHES over the head with the baseball bat, causing a severe injury. HERBERT has been charged with a s. 18 wounding under the Offences Against the Person Act 1861.

Given that the offence charged is one of 'specific intent' can HERBERT rely on the defence of voluntary intoxication?

A No, voluntary intoxication can never be a defence.
B Yes, voluntary intoxication is always a defence for 'specific intent' crimes.
C Yes, provided he can show he could not form the 'specific intent' whilst intoxicated.
D No, in these circumstances he could not use this defence.

Question 3

THOMPSON has been charged with an offence of murder for killing her husband during a domestic dispute and wishes to claim the defence of insanity. She claims that at the time of committing the offence she was suffering from 'a disease of the mind'.

Who must decide the question of whether THOMPSON was suffering from 'a disease of the mind'?

A The judge, as it is a question of law.
B The jury, as it is a question of fact.
C Any doctor, as it is a question of medical opinion.
D A psychologist, as it is a question of specialist medical opinion.

Question 4

DUGGAN, a law lecturer, has been stopped by Constable GARDNER to check his driving documents. During the stop, Constable GARDNER believes she can smell alcohol and requests a breath test. DUGGAN takes the test which is positive and the officer arrests him. DUGGAN says 'that took longer than 40 seconds to go red, your arrest is unlawful' and tries to leave. The officer stops him and DUGGAN punches her. DUGGAN is charged with an offence of assault with intent to resist arrest. DUGGAN says in interview that he honestly, but mistakenly, believed that the arrest was unlawful.

Considering this offence only, could DUGGAN avail himself of the defence of mistake?

A Yes, provided his belief genuinely held.
B Yes, as what he did was 'inadvertent'.
C Yes, provided he could show his actions were 'reasonable'.
D No, in these circumstances the defence would not be available.

Question 5

NEWMAN, aged 15, has been bullied at school by a gang of youths. The gang are well known for shoplifting in the lunch hour in the local shops. One evening, while his parents were out, NEWMAN received a phone call from one of the gang members, stating that the gang wanted him to steal a pair of trainers from a sports shop on the way into school. The caller stated that if he did not comply, he would be severely beaten the next day in school by members of the gang. NEWMAN was very scared and the next day tried to steal a pair of trainers.

In relation to any possible defence that NEWMAN might have, which of the following is correct?

A NEWMAN would not be able to rely on the defence of duress in these circumstances, as it applies to threats of death only.
B Provided NEWMAN held a genuine belief that he would be seriously injured if he did not commit the crime, he would have a defence of duress in these circumstances.
C NEWMAN would be able to rely on the defence of duress in these circumstances, as a threat was made. It is immaterial whether he believed the threat or not.
D NEWMAN would not be able to rely on the defence of duress in these circumstances, as the threat was not immediate.

Question 6

BREWSTER is a member of a gang who, to his knowledge, use loaded firearms to carry out robberies on sub-post offices. The other gang members discuss a forthcoming robbery, and BREWSTER is aware of the plan. During the robbery another member of the gang shoots and kills the sub-post master and they all make good their escape. BREWSTER is later caught and charged with robbery. BREWSTER wishes to use the defence of duress. He claims his wife was threatened at gunpoint after he tried to pull out of the robbery, and he only took part fearing for his wife's life.

Will BREWSTER be allowed to use duress as a defence?

A Yes, as his wife's life was threatened.
B No, the defence will not be available in these circumstances.
C No, the threat must have been against BREWSTER's life.
D Yes, provided the person who issued the threat was the one who shot the sub-post master.

Question 7

BEVAN parks his car whilst he goes into a restaurant for a meal. He meets a friend and ends up drinking more than he had intended. Believing he would be over the legal limit for driving, BEVAN returns to his car to collect his laptop computer, fully intending to get a taxi. There is now a large gang near his car. The gang are very aggressive and BEVAN fears for his personal safety. As they charge at him, he jumps into his car and drives away. He stops about half a mile further down the road, and parks the car, intending to take a taxi. However, a police officer sees BEVAN and breathalyses him, the result of which is positive. BEVAN is charged with a drink driving offence.

Will BEVAN have a defence to this offence?

A Yes, he could claim duress.
B Yes, he could claim duress of circumstances.
C No, there is no defence to drink driving offences.
D No, general defences apply to criminal offences only.

Question 8

KENDAL has been charged with murder. The circumstances are that whilst engaged in a violent struggle with PEARCE, he struck him with a hammer which caused injuries that led to PEARCE's death. KENDAL is claiming self-defence on the grounds that he had an honestly held belief that the force he used was reasonable in all the circumstances.

If KENDAL's defence succeeds what will be the outcome at court?
A He will be not guilty of murder, but guilty of manslaughter.
B He will be guilty of murder, but have a greatly reduced sentence.
C He will be not guilty of murder, nor any other lesser offence.
D He will be not guilty of murder, and re-tried for manslaughter.

Question 9

Constable EAST is on the tactical firearms unit, and has been called to a hostage situation. Unfortunately, the incident ends when Constable EAST fatally shoots RICHARDS, who was the assailant.

In relation to the lawfulness of EAST's use of lethal force, what test will be applied?
A That he had an honestly held belief that it was necessary.
B That such force was reasonable in the circumstances.
C That such force was no more than absolutely necessary.
D That such force was necessary to protect the life of another.

ANSWERS

Question 1

Answer **C** — the defence of automatism applies only where the loss of control is *total*, which makes answers A and B incorrect. The example in the Manual is where a swarm of bees flew into a car causing the driver to lose control (*Hill* v *Baxter* [1958] 1 QB 277). In the circumstances of the question, a temporary loss of concentration caused by the driver trying to swat the bee, could not be seen to be a total loss of control as is required for the defence to succeed. This defence does not involve any foresight to certain risks, so answer D is also wrong.

Question 2

Answer **D** — It is true that voluntary intoxication can sometimes be used as a defence (so answer A is incorrect), even where the crime is one of 'specific intent'. It has been held that where a defendant becomes intoxicated to build up false courage to commit the offence planned, he will not be able to use this defence as he had formed the necessary intent. The intoxication is merely a vehicle to carry out the offence (*Attorney-General for Northern Ireland* v *Gallagher* [1963] AC 349); as he cannot use the defence, answers B and C are incorrect.

Question 3

Answer **A** — The question of whether a person is suffering from 'a disease of the mind' is a question of law, and therefore the judge must decide and not the jury. Therefore, answer B is incorrect. It is not a question of medical opinion, specialist or not (*R* v *Sullivan* [1984] AC 156), making answers C and D incorrect.

Question 4

Answer **D** — The defence of mistake will only be used to negate the *mens rea* of the offence charged. The question is 'did the defendant assault the officer to resist arrest'? The answer is 'yes' and Duggan could not claim to have been 'mistaken' as to whether the officer had a power of arrest or not (*R* v *Lee*, *The Times*, 24 October 2000). However, the defence may have been available had he mistakenly believed the officer was not really a police officer. In the case of *Blackburn* v *Bowering* [1994] 1 WLR 1324, Sir Thomas Bingham said (at p. 1329): 'the important qualification [is] that the mistake must be one of fact (particularly as to the victim's capacity) and not a mistake of law as to the authority of the person acting in that capacity'. So as answers A, B and C all refer to Duggan's belief/actions, they are incorrect as the *mens rea* is clear.

Question 5

Answer **D** — Generally speaking, where a person is threatened with death or serious physical injury unless they carry out a criminal act they may use the defence of duress. However, the threatened injury must be anticipated at or near the time of the offence; not sometime in the future. When a person is threatened with death or serious injury, unless they carry out a criminal act, they may have a defence of duress (see *R* v *Graham* [1982] 1 WLR 294) as it includes serious injury. Therefore, answer A is incorrect. There are, however, caveats to this general use of duress. One of these caveats is that the threatened injury must be anticipated at or near the time of the offence (i.e. not some time in the distant future). As the threat was for the following day Newman could not use the defence, and answers B and C are both incorrect.

Question 6

Answer B — The defence of duress is not available to a person who joins a violent gang, knowing that they might put pressure on him to commit an offence (*R v Sharp* [1987] QB 853). The question follows the broad outline of *Sharp*. A threat of death or serious harm to a partner may allow the defence of duress (as in *R v Ortiz* (1986) 83 Cr App R 173 where threats to the accused's wife or family were considered to be sufficient). Answers A, C and D all refer to some sort of threat or other, and are made incorrect by the fact that Brewster knew that pressure may be applied to him.

Question 7

Answer B — Duress of circumstances is available in traffic cases, so answers C and D are incorrect. Bevan has to show that his actions were reasonable (*R v Martin* [1989] 1 All ER 652). Here his actions could be regarded as 'reasonable', as he feared for his safety. The fact he stopped soon after supports this claim, and the defence has succeeded in similar circumstances (*DPP v Bell* [1992] RTR 335). Contrast this with *DPP v Jones* [1990] RTR 33, where a similar defence failed because the accused drove all the way home, without even checking whether he was still being chased. The facts of this question would not support a defence of 'duress' as no threat has been made, which is a necessary component of that defence, which makes answer A incorrect.

Question 8

Answer C — The defence either succeeds, in which case the accused is acquitted, or it fails, in which case the accused will be convicted of murder (so answers A and D are incorrect). Where the defence fails, due to excessive force, there is no scope to argue that self-defence reduces the defendant's liability to manslaughter (*R v McInnes* [1971] 1 WLR 1600, confirmed in *R v Clegg* [1995] 1 AC 482), so there will be no reduced sentence making answer B incorrect.

Question 9

Answer C — The test applied under s. 3(1) of the Criminal Law Act 1967 — such force as is reasonable in the circumstances — has been superseded, as far as lethal force is concerned, by Article 2 of the European Convention on Human Rights. Under the Convention the test for such force is now no more than 'absolutely necessary'; in addition it must be strictly proportionate to the legitimate purpose being pursued. Anything other than this strict test will *not* be enough, making answers A, B and D incorrect.

4 Homicide

STUDY PREPARATION

This short chapter contains the law relating to some of the most serious charges a person can face. Although these offences are still relatively rare and are usually dealt with by specialist investigators, it is important to know the constituent elements — particularly as it is often more a case of good fortune which prevents people involved in assaults and woundings from forcing these more serious charges. In addition to the offences themselves, the chapter deals extensively with the special defences associated with an indictment for murder. It is worth noting that there are three different types of manslaughter offences and it is worth learning the differences between them.

QUESTIONS

Question 1

WILSON has had a stormy relationship with his girlfriend, who is now seven months' pregnant. One night in a fit of rage he hits her so hard she falls and bangs her head on the wall. She is taken into hospital and goes into early labour. The child is born alive but dies three days later. When interviewed by police, WILSON admits that his intention was only to cause serious injury to the mother.

Which is the most appropriate charge relating to the death of the baby?

A   Murder.
B   Manslaughter.
C   Grievous bodily harm owing to transferred malice of intention.
D   No offence in relation to the death of the baby.

Question 2

There are three special defences open to a person charged with an offence of murder. Should they be successful, what is the legal effect of these defences?

They would:
A   Allow an acquittal.
B   Allow a conviction of manslaughter.
C   Allow a partly reduced sentence.
D   Allow a greatly reduced sentence.

Question 3

HUSSLEBEE is infuriated that her husband has been having an affair for the last three years and confronts her husband and his lover, MARTIN, whilst they were out on a date. HUSSLEBEE is furious and close to losing restraint; her husband says 'she is far better in bed than you and gives great blow jobs'. MARTIN laughs loudly and points at HUSSLEBEE. Completely losing self-control HUSSLEBEE picks up a wine bottle and hits MARTIN over the head with it. MARTIN subsequently dies from her injuries. HUSSLEBEE is charged with murder.

Considering the defence of provocation for HUSSLEBEE, which of the following is true?
A   She cannot claim 'provocation', as MARTIN did not use words to provoke her.
B   She cannot claim 'provocation', as she did not attack the person who provoked her.
C   She can claim 'provocation', even though she attacked MARTIN for only laughing.
D   She can claim 'provocation by circumstances' due to the circumstances of the affair.

Question 4

AMIR, BROOKES and SHARP decide they want to end their lives and form a written agreement. They intend to shoot each other in a game of Russian roulette which involves loading a gun with four bullets, one of which is a blank. They load the revolver and spin the chamber. AMIR fatally shoots BROOKES in the head, and then SHARP fatally shoots AMIR in the head. SHARP then turns the gun on himself but the next bullet is blank. Thankful to be alive SHARP panics and runs from the scene.

In relation to suicide pacts, if SHARP is to use this as a 'special defence' to murder, which of the following must be shown?

A Only that such a pact existed at the time SHARP shot AMIR.
B That a pact existed and that SHARP intended to shoot himself next.
C That a written agreement existed between AMIR and SHARP.
D That a written agreement existed between all the parties.

Question 5

ARMSTRONG is a well-known drugs dealer. He supplies BROWN with a wrap of heroin, which ARMSTRONG knows is dangerous due to its purity. BROWN goes home and injects the heroin into his vein. The heroin is so pure it kills him.

In relation to ARMSTRONG's conduct, which of the following statements is true?

A It amounts to manslaughter by unlawful act.
B It amounts to manslaughter by gross negligence.
C It does not amount to any offence of homicide.
D It amounts to murder.

Question 6

NEAL and MENDEZ were hunting fanatics. While hunting in the local woods, NEAL thought he would play a joke on MENDEZ. NEAL pointed his rifle at MENDEZ, believing there were no bullets in the chamber, and pulled the trigger. However, he had not checked the gun properly and MENDEZ was hit by a bullet in the chest. MENDEZ was taken to the local hospital, where he subsequently died.

In relation to any homicide offences committed by NEAL, which of the following is correct?

A NEAL is guilty of murder in these circumstances, as he was reckless in his actions.
B NEAL is guilty of manslaughter in these circumstances, as he was reckless in his actions.
C NEAL is not guilty of manslaughter by an unlawful act, as he had no intention to injure MENDEZ.
D NEAL is guilty of manslaughter in these circumstances, as he was negligent in relation to his gun.

Question 7

BRANDRICK has been charged with an offence of attempted murder. What is the *mens rea* required to support such a charge?

A Intention to kill the victim.
B Intention to cause grievous bodily harm.
C Intention *either* to kill the victim or to cause grievous bodily harm.
D Recklessness as to whether the victim dies or not.

ANSWERS

Question 1

Answer **B** — The House of Lords decided in *Attorney-General's Reference (No. 3 of 1994)* [1998] AC 245 that the unborn child is not simply a part of its mother but that they are distinct organisms. They also held, however, that the doctrine of transferred malice does not fully apply and therefore answer C is incorrect. An intention to inflict grievous bodily harm on the mother cannot attract liability for murder in respect of the subsequent death of the child (answer A is incorrect) although there will still be a liability for the death of the child, answer D is therefore incorrect. If the intention was to kill the mother and to cause the child to die after having been born alive, there may be an offence of murder but we are not told this in the facts given.

Question 2

Answer **B** — There are three special defences to murder and all three are governed by the Homicide Act 1957. All three are partial defences, reducing the offence from murder to manslaughter rather than leading to an outright acquittal. Answer A is therefore incorrect. These defences are needed principally because the mandatory life sentence for murder does not leave any discretion to the judge in sentencing whereby he or she can take account of factors such as provocation, as would normally be the case with lesser offences where the sentence is not fixed by law. Consequently, answers C and D are incorrect.

Question 3

Answer **C** — Note this question asks you if she can claim the defence of provocation, not whether it will succeed or not. You are not asked to judge that 'a reasonable person' would have acted as HUSSLEBEE did. What is important is that she had a sudden loss of control (the question tells you that) and that there was 'provocation'.

First, provocation is no longer restricted to 'some act, or series of acts', since s. 3 Homicide Act 1957, by its use of the phrase 'whether by things done or by things said or by both together', clearly visualises that words alone can constitute provocation (see *DPP* v *Camplin* [1978] AC 705 per Lord Diplock at p. 716). The acts, words, or indeed sounds, may even be perfectly lawful or commonplace ones as, for example, the crying of a young baby *R* v *Doughty* (1986) 83 Cr App R 319; therefore, answer A is incorrect.

Secondly, it appears it no longer need be 'something done by the dead man to the accused'. It may be something done by a third person in some way connected with the victim (see *R* v *Davies* [1975] QB 691, conduct by wife's lover relevant to whether husband provoked to kill his wife); therefore, answer B is incorrect. Provocation, however, does seem to require conduct on the part of someone, and there is no such thing as provocation by circumstances (*R* v *Acott* [1997] 1 WLR 306). Therefore, answer D is incorrect.

Question 4

Answer **B** — A suicide pact is formed when a common agreement is made between two or more persons, having for its object the death of all of them. It does not have to be written, but does have to be an agreement between all involved. A suicide pact allows for a conviction of manslaughter, and not murder, where the accused was acting in pursuance of such a pact.

The defendant must show that a suicide pact had been made, *and* he or she had the intention of dying at the time the killing took place. (Therefore, answers C and D are incorrect.)

This means that the existence of the pact is not enough (answer A is therefore incorrect) — at the time of the killing there must also be an intention of dying.

Question 5

Answer C — As a starting point you should ask, 'Was the dealer's intention to kill or cause grievous bodily harm to the user?'. If not, the offence of murder will not be made out and therefore answer D is incorrect. Manslaughter by gross negligence requires a degree of negligence by the accused. Here Armstrong was not negligent in supplying the drugs, nor when Brown injected himself (therefore answer B is incorrect). The actions of the user (the self injection) breaks the chain of causation between the unlawful supply and the cause of the death and therefore the dealer is not responsible for the death of the user (*R* v *Dalby* [1982] 1 WLR 62 and *R* v *Armstrong* [1989] Crim LR 149) — answer A is incorrect.

Question 6

Answer **C** — Like most offences, homicide requires that the defendant had the required *mens rea* for the relevant 'unlawful act', which for homicide offences would lead to the death of a victim. If the defendant did not have that *mens rea*, the offence of manslaughter will not be made out and therefore answers A, B and D are incorrect. In the case of *R v Lamb* [1967] 2 QB 981, the defendant pretended to fire a revolver at his friend. Although the defendant believed that the weapon would not fire, the chamber containing a bullet moved round to the firing pin and the defendant's friend was killed. As Lamb did not have the *mens rea* required for an assault his conviction for manslaughter was quashed.

Question 7

Answer **A** — According to CPS Charging Standards, para. 10.3, 'unlike murder, which requires an intention to kill or cause grievous bodily harm, attempted murder requires evidence of an intention to kill alone'. Thus an intention to kill is the required *mens rea* for this offence and therefore answers B, C and D are incorrect.

5 Misuse of Drugs

STUDY PREPARATION

Offences relating to the misuse of drugs require a sound knowledge both of the elements of the offences and the case law that supports them. You should also understand the elements of the statutory defences that apply, and how they affect the case in question. This chapter also covers the rather complicated power to enter, search and seize granted by s. 23 of the Misuse of Drugs Act 1971, and it is well worth taking your time over this section (if you've read it you'll know what I mean!). In addition to the more usual controlled drugs, this chapter also includes the law relating to intoxicating substances.

QUESTIONS

Question 1

Constable FOSTER asks your advice regarding the offence of supplying articles for administration or preparing controlled drugs (contrary to s. 9A of the Misuse of Drugs Act 1971). She has received information regarding HAINING, who is supplying hypodermic syringes to drug users who are using them to inject themselves with heroin. Constable FOSTER asks you what action she can take.

In relation to the above offence, which of the following is correct?

A Constable FOSTER can apply for a search warrant under the 1971 Act.
B Constable FOSTER can arrest HAINING for committing the offence.
C Constable FOSTER can report HAINING for committing the offence.
D The offence is not complete; hypodermic syringes are not included in this offence.

Misuse of Drugs 37

Question 2

GOSS has a bottle of vitamin tablets in her handbag. Unknown to her, her son had put three Ecstasy tablets in the bottle that morning. Before leaving the house GOSS checks that she has the bottle in her handbag.

Which of the following is correct?
A GOSS is in possession of a controlled drug, but may not be committing an offence.
B GOSS is in possession of a controlled drug and is committing an offence.
C OSS is not in possession of a controlled drug as she did not put them in the bottle.
D GOSS is not in possession of a controlled drug as she has no knowledge of what they are.

Question 3

Detective Constable JONES is a member of the National Crime Squad. She has been involved in an undercover operation in relation to drug trafficking. STEER is a major drug dealer and has asked JONES to help in the supply of cocaine. JONES has provisionally agreed to this to maintain her cover. In fact JONES has no intention of illegally supplying drugs, and an arrest of STEER is imminent.

In relation to incitement under s. 19 of the Misuse of Drugs Act 1971, which of the following is correct?
A The offence is complete when STEER asks JONES to supply the drugs.
B As JONES has no intention of supplying the drugs, the offence is not complete.
C The offence would be complete only if JONES actually supplied the drugs.
D The offence is complete only if STEER receives the drugs, and supplying is complete.

Question 4

PATEL is a self-employed chemist and her partner, NEWMAN, confessed to her that he was a heroin addict, although not registered as such. PATEL was shocked by the news, but agreed to help NEWMAN break his addiction. PATEL took some methadone from her storeroom, and gave it to NEWMAN.

In relation to PATEL's actions, which of the following is incorrect?
A PATEL has committed no offence in these circumstances, as she had lawful possession of the drug.

B Even though PATEL would normally be entitled to lawfully possess a controlled drug, she has committed an offence by supplying it to NEWMAN.
C PATEL has committed an offence in these circumstances.
D PATEL has committed an offence from the time she took the drug from the surgery intending to supply it to NEWMAN.

Question 5

Consider the following situations. In which, if any, will MEREDITH be able to claim a statutory defence to the offence of possession of a controlled drug?
1. She finds white powder, which she believes is cocaine, in her son's room. She takes it intending to flush it down the toilet. However, as a leader of the local youth club, she decides to keep it to show her co-leaders so they will be able to recognise the drug should they find any.
2. She finds a quantity of ecstasy tablets, which she buries in the back garden hoping nature will take its course and destroy the drugs.

A Situation 1 only.
B Situation 2 only.
C Both Situations.
D Neither situation.

Question 6

HAMMOND is a customs officer working undercover. She is part of an on-going operation regarding drug supply at the 'Green Man' public house. The officer goes to the pub to make a test purchase, and is shown several wraps containing white powder by HAYES, a suspected drug dealer. HAYES states that the wraps contain amphetamine and will cost £30 per wrap. In fact the wraps contain baking powder, a fact of which HAYES is unaware. The transaction takes place.

Which of the following offences, if any, does HAYES commit?
A Possession of a controlled drug.
B Possession with intent to supply a controlled drug.
C Offering to supply a controlled drug.
D Supplying a controlled drug.

Question 7

BARTON and HOLLOWAY are business partners. HOLLOWAY uses her factory for the production of Ecstasy. BARTON ensures that the premises are not disturbed by providing 24-hour security in the factory, and also provides transportation to the factory of the raw goods required for the production of Ecstasy. BARTON neither visits the factory, nor has any direct contact with the security or transportation, but is aware of what happens at the factory. HOLLOWAY never visits the factory either.

Who, if anyone, is guilty of unlawful production of a controlled drug contrary to s. 4 of the Misuse of Drugs Act 1971?

A BARTON.
B HOLLOWAY.
C Both of them.
D Neither of them.

Question 8

BOOKER has long been suspected by the police of being involved in the supply of controlled drugs and a warrant has been obtained to search his premises. The police go to BOOKER's house and, as they enter, BOOKER takes various papers and shreds them. BOOKER is unsure whether they are evidence or not, but is not willing to take a chance. These papers actually amounted to the only real evidence proving BOOKER's involvement in the supply of controlled drugs.

Has BOOKER committed an offence of obstruction contrary to s. 23(4) of the Misuse of Drugs Act 1971?

A Yes, he was reckless as to whether the papers were evidence or not.
B Yes, he has obstructed the officers by destroying the evidence.
C No, as obstruction only applies to deliberate, physical obstruction of the officers themselves.
D No, as obstruction only applies to stop/searches in relation to drugs.

Question 9

Police officers involved in intelligence operations may have to commit acts that are unlawful by virtue of the Misuse of Drugs Act 1971. The officers, as well as other professionals, are exempted from the 1971 Act by the Misuse of Drugs Regulations 2001.

In relation to these exemptions, which if either of the following statements is/are correct?

1. Police officers may keep controlled drugs in their possession.
2. Police officers may supply controlled drugs to another.

A Statement 1 only.
B Statement 2 only.

C Both statements.
D Neither statement.

Question 10

GORDON has a controlled drug in his pocket, which he intends to supply to someone else. Seeing a police officer in the distance, he hands the drugs to his friend, MEREDITH, and says 'hold on to these for me and I will give you £20'. MEREDITH agrees and takes possession of the drugs. The officer walks past them and MEREDITH hands the drugs back to GORDON and collects his £20.

In relation to the controlled drugs, which offence(s) has MEREDITH committed?

A Possession only.
B Supply only.
C Possession or supplying only.
D Possession or supplying or possession with intent to supply.

Question 11

GOULD is 16 years old and works on Saturdays in his father's shop. He sells a bottle of solvent to his school friend whom he knows is 16 years old. Under s. 1 of the Intoxicating Substances (Supply) Act 1985 (supply of an intoxicating substance), which of the following is correct in relation to the defences available to GOULD?

A GOULD has a defence owing to his age only.
B GOULD has a defence as he was acting in the course of a business.
C GOULD has a defence owing to his age and the fact that he was acting in the course of a business.
D GOULD has no defence.

Question 12

LAING was in possession of cocaine, which he firmly believed to be amphetamine. He is supplying the drug, and has clingfilm, scales and paper on him to assist in this supply.

Considering the offence of possession with intent to supply (s. 5(3) Misuse of Drugs Act 1971), which of the following is correct?

A The prosecution must prove that it was a controlled drug and that he knew it was a controlled drug.

B The prosecution must prove that is was cocaine, and that LAING suspected that is was cocaine.
C The paraphernalia in his possession is evidence of his intention to supply.
D It is immaterial that he thought it was some other type of drug; possession with intent is enough.

Question 13

A travel restriction order made under the Criminal Justice and Police Act 2001 to restrict the travel of convicted drug traffickers lasts for a maximum of what period?

A Two years.
B Four years.
C Ten years.
D Unlimited period; no set maximum.

ANSWERS

Question 1

Answer **D** — This offence deals with the supplying of or offering to supply articles for use for preparing or administering controlled drugs. The offence is designed to address the provision of drug 'kits'. It specifically does not include hypodermic syringes, or parts of them (s. 9A(2)). The administration for which the articles are intended must be 'unlawful'. As the offence has not been committed, there is no action that the officer can take to either search or bring HAINING before justice and therefore answers A, B and C are incorrect. The offence has no specific power of arrest.

Question 2

Answer **A** — Common law outlines possession as physical control plus knowledge of the presence of the drugs. This becomes problematical where the person in possession claims not to realise what they possessed. In these cases you need to show that the person had physical control of the container together with knowledge that it contained something. GOSS knew she had a container and that it contained tablets (answers C and D are therefore incorrect). This simply means that GOSS was in possession of controlled drugs, not that she was committing an offence under the 1971

Act. As answer C states she is committing an offence for simply possessing the drugs, it is incorrect. She may commit an offence, as outlined in answer A; however, she could avail herself of the statutory defences available.

Question 3

Answer **A** — The definition of this offence under s. 19 of the Misuse of Drugs Act 1971 is 'for a person to incite . . . another to commit [an offence under this Act]'. This clearly covers all sections, not just supplying.

Although the offence of incitement exists for most other offences generally (see Chapter 3), the 1971 Act makes a specific offence of inciting another to commit an offence under its provisions.

On the arguments in *DPP* v *Armstrong* [2000] Crim LR 379, it would seem that a person inciting an undercover police officer may commit an offence under this section even though there was no possibility of the officer actually being induced to commit the offence and therefore answer B is incorrect. As the offence is committed at the time the incitement is made and is not conditional on either the supply or receipt of the controlled drugs, answers C and D are incorrect.

Question 4

Answer **A** — Section 5 of the Misuse of Drugs Act 1971 states:

> (3) Subject to section 28 of this Act, it is an offence for a person to have a controlled drug in his possession, whether lawfully or not, with intent to supply it to another in contravention of section 4(1) of this Act.

It is important to note that the lawfulness or otherwise of the possession is irrelevant; what matters here is the lawfulness of the intended supply. If a vet or a police officer or some other person is in lawful possession of a controlled drug but they intend to supply it unlawfully to another, this offence will be made out.

This is a crime of specific intent and the intention to supply would have to be proven, as it is in the question. Consequently, PATEL commits an offence, making answers B, C and D actually correct in law. The question, though, asks you what is incorrect and therefore answer A is actually the correct answer.

Question 5

Answer **D** — Defences are provided by s. 5 of the Misuse of Drugs Act 1971 which states:

(4) In any proceedings for an offence under subsection (2) above in which it is proved that the accused had a controlled drug in his possession, it shall be a defence for him to prove —
 (a) that, knowing or suspecting it to be a controlled drug he took possession of it for the purpose of preventing another from committing or continuing to commit an offence in connection with that drug and that as soon as possible after taking possession of it he took all such steps as were reasonably open to him to destroy the drug or to deliver it into the custody of a person lawfully entitled to take custody of it; or
 (b) that, knowing or suspecting it to be a controlled drug he took possession of it for the purpose of delivering it into the custody of a person lawfully entitled to take custody of it and that as soon as possible after taking possession of it he took all such steps as were reasonably open to him to deliver it into the custody of such a person.

In the first situation, having taken initial steps to destroy the drug, Meredith could claim a defence under subsection (4)(a). However, when she then decides to keep the cocaine she loses that right and would be in unlawful possession. Consequently, as situation 1 does not give rise to a defence, answers A and C are incorrect. In the second situation, which is a fairly technical issue in relation to the defence, the Administrative Court supported the view that relying on the forces of nature did not provide this defence (*R v Murphy* [2002] EWCA Crim 1587). At the original trial of the accused for burying cannabis the trial judge had not left it open to the jury to consider the defence, and even on appeal this approach was endorsed. Consquently, situation 2 does not give rise to a defence and answer B is also incorrect.

Question 6

Answer C — For the offence of possession, possession with intent to supply and supply, the prosecution would need to prove that the substance in question is in fact a controlled drug. Answers A, B and D are therefore incorrect. For the offence of offering to supply, it does not matter whether the accused had a controlled drug in his or her possession or had easy access to a controlled drug.

Question 7

Answer C — The meaning of 'produce' and 'concerned in production' is defined by s. 37 of the Misuse of Drugs Act 1971 which states:

(1) ... 'produce', where the reference is to producing a controlled drug, means producing it by manufacture, cultivation or any other method, and 'production' has a corresponding meaning; ...

Being concerned in production requires the accused to take an identifiable role in the production. Both BARTON and HOLLOWAY take an identifiable role in the production in that, although they never visit the premises, they have guilty knowledge of its function and, but for their actions, the production may not take place. This makes option C the only possible correct answer.

Question 8

Answer **B** — This offence is complete where the person obstructs someone carrying out stop/search procedures and also executing a warrant and therefore answer D is incorrect. In *R v Forde* (1985) 81 Cr App R 19, it was held that a person only committed this offence if the obstruction was intentional, that is to say the act viewed objectively, through the eyes of a bystander, did obstruct the constable's search, and viewed subjectively, that is to say through the eyes of the accused himself, was intended so to obstruct. BOOKER knew he was intentionally obstructing the officers and even though he was unsure of the outcome recklessness does not apply (answer A is incorrect). Section 23(4)(b) of the Misuse of Drugs Act 1971 states that the offence includes a person who 'conceals from a person acting in the exercise of his powers under subsection (1) above any such books, documents . . .'. So as books and documents are included, answer C is incorrect.

Question 9

Answer **C** — Regulation 6 of the Misuse of Drugs Regulations 2001 provides that certain people, including police officers in the course of their duty, may possess and supply controlled drugs to others under very strict conditions. Both these statements are correct and as such answers A, B and D are incorrect.

Question 10

Answer **D** — In its simplest form, where one person hands over a controlled drug to another, there can be said to be a supply. Where a person leaves a controlled drug with another for safekeeping, the situation is trickier. Fortunately, the House of Lords have given direction in this area in two cases: *R v Maginnis* [1987] AC 303 and *R v Dempsey* Dempsey and Dempsey (1986) 82 Cr App R 291. The outcome of these cases is that if the person looking after the drugs for another is in some way benefiting from that activity, then the return of those drugs to the depositor *will* amount to 'supplying' and the offences supplying or possession with intent to supply will be applicable as well as simple possession. None of these offences need stand alone in the circumstances outlined in the question and therefore answers A, B and C are incorrect.

Question 11

Answer **D** — Section 1 of the Intoxicating Substances (Supply) Act 1985 defines the defence in subsection (2) as:

> in proceedings against any person for an offence under subsection (1) above it is a defence for him to show that at the time he made the supply or offer he was under the age of 18 and was acting otherwise than in the course or furtherance of a business.

So on one hand GOULD does have a defence in that he is 16, but this does not stand alone as the statute says 'under the age of 18 *and*', that 'and' makes answer A incorrect. The second part of the subsection concerns 'acting otherwise than in the course or furtherance of a business' and as GOULD was so doing, answers B and C are incorrect.

Question 12

Answer **D** — The prosecution only has to establish that the accused was in possession of the controlled drug as charged with the necessary intent. The accused will not be able to avail himself of the defences in s. 28(2) or 28(3)(b)(ii) where he believed the substance to be a different drug from that alleged by the prosecution as it is not necessary for the prosecution to prove which controlled drug it was in order to obtain a conviction (*R* v *Leeson* [2000] 1 Cr App Rep 233); therefore, answers A and B are incorrect. Although possession of drugs paraphernalia will be relevant evidence to show a tendency to be involved in drugs dealing, it does not prove the intention to supply, and careful direction by the judge is needed in outlining it's probative value (*R* v *Haye* [2002] EWCA Crim 2476); therefore, answer C is incorrect.

Question 13

Answer **D** — The introduction of the Criminal Justice and Police Act 2001, ss. 33–37, allows any criminal court (but, effectively giving the sentencing restriction, this means the Crown Court) to impose a travel restriction order on an offender who is convicted of a drug trafficking offence. The offender has to have been sentenced by that court to a term of imprisonment for four years or more (s. 33(1)). The effect of the order is to restrict the offender's freedom to leave the United Kingdom for a period specified by the court, and it may require delivery up of his passport. The minimum duration of a travel restriction order is two years, starting from the date of the offender's release from custody. There is no maximum period prescribed in the legislation, therefore answers A, B and C are incorrect. The court must always consider whether such an order should be made and must give reasons where it does not consider such an order to be appropriate (s. 33(2)).

6 Offences Arising Out of Pregnancy and Childbirth

STUDY PREPARATION

Thankfully, most officers will never deal with any of the offences outlined in this chapter. Nevertheless, for the sake of completeness in covering the law relating to assaults, battery and homicide, it is important to understand how these areas fit in. The subject of abortion carries with it strong feelings and emotions. Although individual views vary greatly the legal issues are relatively clear — if not universally supported.

The coming into force of the Human Rights Act 1998 reinforced an individual's right to life, along with a positive obligation on the State to protect that right. Even though the European Court of Human Rights has made a number of clear rulings on the area of abortion, the 1998 Act may be instrumental in the development of this emotive area.

QUESTIONS

Question 1

STUBBS, a married woman, has been having an affair. Having missed her period she believes she may be pregnant. She does not wish her husband to find out and asks her brother, who is a pharmacist, to give her something to induce an abortion. Her brother produces a mixture with which he intends to induce an abortion and STUBBS drinks it. However, as she is not in fact pregnant, the mixture has no effect.

> Have either STUBBS or her brother committed an offence contrary to s. 58 of the Offences against the Person Act 1861 relating to abortion?

A Full offence by STUBBS, an attempt by her brother.
B An attempt by STUBBS, full offence by her brother.
C An attempt by both as she is not pregnant.
D Neither commit any offence as she is not pregnant.

Question 2

Amy, who is 15 years old, secretly gives birth to a child. Desperate to hide this fact from her parents, she takes the child to the local park and hides it under a bush. The child lives for a few hours, but dies of hypothermia.

At which point, if any, does Amy commit the offence of concealing the birth?
A As soon as she forms the intention to conceal the birth.
B As soon as she hides the child in the bushes.
C As soon as the child dies.
D She does not commit this offence.

Question 3

THOMPSON's wife gives birth to a child, but dies during labour. THOMPSON is overcome with grief on the death of his wife and the balance of his mind is disturbed by this traumatic incident. He has not fully recovered from this when he takes the child home, and is so traumatised he blames the child for the death. THOMPSON deliberately does not feed or look after the child and it dies.

Is THOMPSON guilty of infanticide?
A No, as infanticide only relates to wilful acts, not omissions.
B No, the offence can only be committed by the child's mother.
C Yes, provided he can show the balance of his mind was disturbed.
D Yes, as the act allows wilful omissions to be considered.

Question 4

'Legal' abortion can be carried out on a pregnancy that has not exceeded what period?
A 22 weeks.
B 24 weeks.
C 26 weeks.
D 28 weeks.

Question 5

STRUTHERS goes to MILLS's flat in connection with a proposed abortion. There was a pan on the stove containing various instruments, which undoubtedly could be used for the purpose of procuring an abortion. MILLS stated that he was boiling the instruments to sterilize them before performing the abortion, having obtained them from his friend for such purpose.

> Dealing only with supplying or procuring means for abortion under s. 59 of the Offences Against the Person Act 1861 at what point, if any, would MILLS commit the offence?

A Only if MILLS went on to use the instruments to perform the abortion.
B When he begins to sterilize the instruments for the procedure.
C When he obtains the instruments from his friend.
D When he agrees with STRUTHERS to perform the procedure.

ANSWERS

Question 1

Answer **B** — The full offence is committed by a woman who *must be* pregnant, therefore answer A is incorrect. However, this is not necessary where another person is charged with the offence and therefore answers C and D are incorrect as her brother could commit the substantive offence. As the offence is indictable, Stubbs may well be guilty of attempting the offence, even if she was acting on her own, particularly as she has clearly acted in a way that is more than merely preparatory to the commission of the substantive offence.

Question 2

Answer **D** — The accused's act must be done in relation to a dead body, so that the offence is not committed where the accused conceals a living child which later dies. As the statute says, 'secret disposition of the dead body of the sad child'. Therefore, answers A, B and C are incorrect. An alternative and more appropriate charge would appear to be some form of homicide in relation to the initial act of concealing the living child which led to its death.

Question 3

Answer B — The offence predates the introduction of the defence of diminished responsibility and is designed to serve a similar role in relation to killings of very young children by their *mothers* in circumstances where they are not fully responsible for their actions. Answers A, C and D are therefore incorrect.

Although it does include wilful omissions, the offence does not extend to fathers traumatised by events. Here the only charge could be murder; however, a defence of diminished responsibility could be available.

Question 4

Answer B — There is a fixed time-limit of 24 weeks for abortions under s. 1(1)(a) of the Abortion Act 1967, but no time-limit at all (up to the point of a live birth) under s. 1(1)(b), (c) or (d). Also note that the opinion, formed in good faith, of two medical practitioners is required except where necessary to save the life of the woman or to prevent injury to her physical or mental health. Consequently, answers A, C and D are incorrect.

Question 5

Answer C — This offence requires supply or procuring of instruments for the purpose of procuring a miscarriage of any woman; simple possession is not enough. 'Supply' means supply to another, and conversely 'procure' means procure from another, i.e. 'get possession of something of which you do not have possession already' (R v *Mills* [1963] 1 QB 522). The offence is complete when Mills 'procured' the instruments with knowledge of their intended use. The act of sterilizing them, or using them does not make out this offence (answers A and B are incorrect), and more than an agreement is needed (answer D is incorrect).

7 Offences Against the Person

STUDY PREPARATION

This chapter deals with all non-fatal offences against the person, combining the relevant chapters of the *Blackstone's Police Manual*. This chapter examines the definition of assault and battery; it also addresses the offences of common assault, actual and grievous bodily harm and the differences between them. Of particular importance in this area is the required element of state of mind (*mens rea*) and how that differs between offences.

Specific assaults in relation to police officers are considered, along with the less common offences of torture and poisoning. This chapter also covers the very serious offences of false imprisonment, kidnapping and hostage-taking. Although infrequently charged, these offences are perhaps of greater significance in the light of recent terrorist activity. This chapter should be read in conjunction with CPS Charging Standards.

QUESTIONS

Question 1

GRAHAM has been lawfully arrested for an assault where he punched a neighbour. The matter has been investigated and a charge of common assault is being laid. What should the charge outline in relation to the offence?

A Assault and battery.
B Assault by battery.
C Assault or battery.
D Assault by beating.

Question 2

In considering the legal definition of assault, which of the following is correct?
A There must be intention to cause fear, although actual fear need not be proven.
B There can be recklessness as to fear caused and actual fear need not be proven.
C There must be fear of force being used, even though it may not be immediate.
D There must be fear of force being used and it must be immediate.

Question 3

DOUGHERTY takes her children to their dentist, WALKER. She consents to the children receiving fillings. During the procedure DOUGHERTY becomes concerned that WALKER is either drunk or drugged and reports the matter to the police. During the investigation is transpires that WALKER is taking drugs prescribed for a psychiatric illness, and for that reason he was suspended by the General Dental Council two months ago. The police are considering charging WALKER with assault.

Has WALKER unlawfully assaulted the children?
A No, DOUGHERTY has given true consent.
B No, any formal medical practice is not an assault.
C Yes, DOUGHERTY has given consent obtained by fraud.
D Yes, WALKER is suspended and no longer covered by law as it relates to consent.

Question 4

Constable MAHONEY is on patrol when she sees GRAHAM punch ANDREWS in the face. The officer intervenes. However, ANDREWS states he is not interested in taking action. Constable MAHONEY decides to report GRAHAM for summons for the offence of common assault. At court, the magistrates decide that although proven, the assault is so trifling that it did not merit any punishment. In relation to a 'certificate of disposal' which of the following is true?
A It may not be issued as the case was proven.
B It may not be issued as the case was not brought by ANDREWS.
C It may be issued but ANDREWS could take further civil action against GRAHAM.
D It may be issued and ANDREWS could not take further action against GRAHAM.

Question 5

SWALES is a store detective employed by a major retail chain. He witnesses a theft of a £200 cashmere sweater and follows the suspect, GRAINGER, outside the shop.

SWALES holds GRAINGER and asks him to return to the shop as he has items for which he has not paid. GRAINGER pulls a knife and threatens SWALES with it. SWALES backs off and GRAINGER makes good his escape.

Has GRAINGER committed an offence of assault with intent to resist arrest contrary to s. 38 of the Offences Against the Person Act 1861?
A No, as it applies to police officers making arrests only.
B No, as it applies to assaults involving actual injury only.
C Yes, as it applies to arrests made by any citizen, not just police officers.
D Yes, provided it was proved that GRAINGER suspected he was being arrested.

Question 6

Constable DOUGHTY wishes to question MILLS about an alleged assault. The officer attends at MILLS's home address and tells him the nature of the incident. Knowing that he is about to be arrested, MILLS grabs hold of Constable DOUGHTY's arm and pulls him into the doorway; he then slams the door on the officer's arm and makes good his escape. As a result of this attack, Constable DOUGHTY's arm is broken in two places. When, interviewed, MILLS states that he did not intend to cause the injury, but accepts that his conduct presented a risk of some harm to the officer.

Which of the following statements is correct?
A This would not amount to a s. 18 assault, as there was no malice, i.e. premeditation.
B This would not amount to a s. 18 assault, as there was no intention to cause serious harm.
C This would amount to a s. 18 assault, as MILLS intended to prevent his lawful arrest.
D This would not amount to a s. 18 assault, as MILLS had not actually been arrested.

Question 7

PEARSON suspects that his wife is having an affair, as she goes out every Friday and Saturday night. She denies the allegation and intends to go out with her friends this Friday. When Friday comes PEARSON follows her into town, goes into the club she is in, grabs hold of her and takes her back to his car about 100 metres down the road. His wife breaks free and runs back to her friends.

Has PEARSON committed the offence of kidnapping?
A No, as he only took her a short way.

B No, you cannot kidnap your spouse.
C No, he commits the offence of false imprisonment.
D Yes, all the elements of the offence are met.

Question 8

REES has had enough of her neighbour PATEY playing loud music at all hours of the day and night. One morning she took PATEY's milk from his doorstep. REES crushed eight sleeping tablets prescribed for her own use and put them in the milk returning the bottle to PATEY's doorstep. REES knew exactly what she was doing and intended to make PATEY ill. The effects of the tablets were reduced by the milk, however, and simply made PATEY fall asleep.

Has REES committed the offence of poisoning with intent contrary to s. 24 of the Offences Against the Person Act 1861?

A Yes, as REES intended to injure, aggrieve or annoy PATEY.
B No, as the drugs are not 'noxious things'.
C Yes, provided that REES was at least reckless to any injury caused.
D No, as PATEY's life was never in danger.

Question 9

VICKERY is the Mayor of a small town and a strong advocate of European monetary union. Whilst leaving the town hall he sees STROUD writing graffiti on the front door. It stated 'you can stick your Euros up your arse Vickery'. Incensed at this criminal damage, VICKERY makes a citizen's arrest and takes his prisoner back up into his office. In there he makes STROUD squat in the corner of his office and leaves him there for an hour. VICKERY then asks all 15 members of staff to come into the room at look at STROUD. They all laugh at him causing him extreme humiliation. VICKERY calls the police and STROUD is arrested for criminal damage.

Which of the following statements is true?

A VICKERY has not committed torture, as there was no real physical suffering by STROUD.
B VICKERY has not committed torture, as he is not acting in the performance of his public duties.
C VICKERY has committed torture, as he is a public official and has subjected STROUD to degrading treatment.
D VICKERY and his staff members have all committed torture.

Question 10

TURNER has fallen out with his girlfriend following a heated argument. He sees her in town one afternoon with another man. TURNER's girlfriend is carrying her two year old son. TURNER punches his girlfriend on the nose, breaking it and making it bleed. At the time she is punched she drops the child, causing cuts and bruises to his face. TURNER then threatens his girlfriend's friend, who fearing for his immediate safety, runs off.

In relation to this action, on whom has TURNER committed battery?

A His girlfriend and her friend.
B Only his girlfriend.
C Both his girlfriend and the child.
D All three of them.

Question 11

STEVENS is having an argument with BRIDGES in the street, opposite the police station. BRIDGES picks up a large piece of wood and raises it above his head. He says to STEVENS, 'How dare you swear at me. If we weren't opposite the nick I'd let you have this'.

Which of the following statements is correct?

A BRIDGES has committed an assault as he threatened to use immediate force.
B BRIDGES has committed an assault as he picked up a weapon.
C BRIDGES has not committed an assault as force was not actually used.
D BRIDGES has not committed an assault as his threat was negated by his words.

Question 12

FAULKNER is a Police Community Support Officer (PCSO) employed by her local Police Authority. Whilst on patrol she meets DALTON who takes exception to her presence and wrestles her to the ground. CONNIKIE, a member of the public and very community minded, tries to pull DALTON off of FAULKNER and DALTON responds by pushing CONNIKIE over.

Which of the following is true in relation to The Police Reform Act 2002?

A DALTON has committed an offence of assaulting a designated or accredited person in relation to both FAULKNER and CONNIKIE and is arrestable.
B DALTON has committed an offence of assaulting a designated or accredited person in relation to FAULKNER only and is arrestable.
C DALTON has committed an offence of assaulting a designated or accredited person in relation to both FAULKNER and CONNIKIE, and there is no power of arrest.

D DALTON has committed an offence of assaulting a designated or accredited person in relation to FAULKNER only, and there is no power of arrest.

ANSWERS

Question 1

Answer **D** — The Divisional Court in *DPP* v *Taylor* [1992] QB 645 has held that all common assaults and batteries are now offences contrary to s. 39 of the Criminal Justice Act 1988, and that the information must include a reference to that section. An information would be bad for duplicity if the phrase 'assault and battery' were used, which makes answers A, B and C all incorrect; the court suggested that 'assault by beating' was the appropriate wording. This advice has been given to all forces by the CPS who recommend that wording as the most appropriate for the charge.

Question 2

Answer **D** — There has to be intentional or reckless causation of the fear of force, but the fear of force is the key to assault, which makes answers A and B incorrect. An assault requires conduct, which causes the victim to apprehend the immediate use of unlawful force upon him. The concept of immediacy has nevertheless been interpreted with some flexibility, and there have been a number of recent cases in which 'stalkers' have been prosecuted for assault on that basis. In *Smith* v *Chief Superintendent, Woking Police Station* (1983) 76 Cr App R 234, the Divisional Court held that a threat of violence could be considered immediate, even though the accused was still outside the victim's home, looking in at her through a window, and would have needed to force an entry before he could attack her. This, however, relates to the time period and not the victim's actual fear, which remains as the fear of immediate use of unlawful force and therefore answer C is incorrect.

Question 3

Answer **A** — This question deals with the question of consent and broadly follows the outline of the circumstances in the case of *R* v *Richardson* [1999] QB 444. In that case it was held that a dentist's failure to inform patients that the General Dental Council had suspended him did not affect the true 'consent' given for medical treatment (answer D is incorrect). In *Richardson* Otton LJ held that there had been no deception as to the identity of the dentist, or the nature of the act carried out, and this therefore could not vitiate consent and there could be no assault. Consent obtained by fraud would relate to the identity of the dentist as a trained dentist, which is not the case here and answer C is therefore incorrect. Consent to medical treatment is true consent, but going beyond agreed treatment could be an assault, e.g. the indecent touching of the patient, and thus answer B is incorrect.

Question 4

Answer B — The certificate of disposal is issued to prevent any further action being taken by the aggrieved against the accused, and as such it must be shown that the victim brought the charge or it was brought on the victim's behalf. As it wasn't in this case, a certificate could not be issued, so answer D is incorrect. It may be issued where the magistrates find the offence not to have been proven, *or* the assault to have been justified, *or* so trifling as not to merit any punishment. Note the use of the term 'or', which makes answer A incorrect. The certificate, if issued, absolves the defendant from further criminal *or* civil action arising from the same facts, so answer C is incorrect.

Question 5

Answer C — On a literal reading of s. 38 of the Offences Against the Person Act 1861, the only *actus reus* required is that of common assault, making answer B incorrect, whereas the *mens rea* is that of common assault, coupled with an intent to resist or prevent one's own, or another person's, lawful arrest or detention. Nevertheless, it is firmly established that the arrest or detention in question must in fact be lawful (*R v Self* [1992] 3 All ER 476; *R v Lee*, [2000] Crim LR 991) and this is an essential element. The person making the arrest (or trying to) need not be a police officer, which makes answer A incorrect. It may be a private citizen assisting such an officer, or a private citizen or store detective making a 'citizen's arrest'.

The accused has no defence if his mistake is merely one of law, as for example where he does not appreciate that a citizen has a power of arrest, or where he assumes that an arrest is unlawful merely because he is (or believes himself to be) innocent of the offence in question. This makes answer D incorrect.

Question 6

Answer C — 'Maliciously' does not need premeditation, but rather amounts to subjective recklessness (*Cunningham* recklessness), and the suspect admits this. He accepts that there was a risk of harm. He does not have to foresee the degree of harm and therefore answer A is incorrect. This offence has two strands: (i) an intention to cause serious harm, or (ii) an intention to resist or prevent lawful apprehension. Where, in contrast, it is alleged that the defendant merely intended to resist arrest

58 Offences Against the Person

etc., malice becomes an important further element to be proved and therefore answer B is incorrect. It applies to intention to prevent, as well as resist arrest, and not just when someone has actually been arrested and therefore D is incorrect.

Question 7

Answer **D** — The offences of false imprisonment, kidnapping and hostage-taking are very closely linked, in fact the state of mind required is the same. In *R v Rahman* (1985) 81 Cr App R 349, it was stated that the *mens rea* for false imprisonment is intentional or reckless restraint of a person's movement (recklessness here means subjective or *Cunningham* recklessness). Answer C is incorrect, as PEARSON has not restrained his wife's movement. You can kidnap your spouse, as you could kidnap any person provided the basic definition of the offence is met (*R v Reid* [1973] QB 299) and therefore answer B is incorrect. Also, the distance taken may only be a short one (*R v Wellard* [1978] 3 All ER 161 and therefore answer A is incorrect.

Question 8

Answer **A** — In the case of *R v Callaghan* [2001] EWCA Crim 198, the court held that administering a drug to another without their knowledge or consent was a 'most serious offence'. The offence is one of specific intent, and recklessness is not sufficient, so answer C is incorrect. In *R v Marcus* [1981] 2 All ER 833, the Court of Appeal held that a substance which might be harmless in small quantities could therefore be 'noxious' if the quantity administered was sufficient to injure, aggrieve or annoy (answer B is incorrect). Section 24 is distinguished from s. 23 of the 1861 Act, in that the latter requires proof of a consequence; namely, the endangering of a person's life or the infliction of grievous bodily harm, and therefore answer D is incorrect.

Question 9

Answer **B** — Vickery does not appear to be acting in the performance or purported performance of his duties, and therefore cannot be guilty of torture (answer C is incorrect). It might be argued that he saw his actions as being part of his civic managerial duties, but this is unlikely to succeed. The meaning of 'severe pain or suffering' does not have to amount to grievous bodily harm, actual bodily harm or any standard measured by degree of injury. Indeed, the wording of s. 134(3) of the Criminal Justice Act 1988 provides that the pain or suffering may be purely mental. It is the severity of the pain rather than whether or not identifiable injury results that should be considered, though evidence of injury would be admissible evidence of the severity of the pain. Answer A is therefore incorrect. The arguments against the actions of

Vickery falling within the scope of his public duties apply even more clearly to the actions of his staff and therefore answer D is also incorrect.

Question 10

Answer C — A battery requires the unlawful application of force upon the victim so, although the male friend has been assaulted, he has not been 'battered'. Answers A and D are therefore wrong. Where someone strikes another causing her to drop and injure her child, it has been held to be a battery against both (*Haystead* v *Chief Constable of Derbyshire* [2000] 3 All ER 890). As the child has also been assaulted, answer B is incorrect.

Question 11

Answer D — Words used by the accused may indicate that no real attack is imminent, even where the circumstances might suggest otherwise. This principle has been clearly established since the very ancient case of *Tuberville* v *Savage* (1669) 1 Mod 3, where in the course of a quarrel with S, T placed his hand on the hilt of his sword (an act which might ordinarily have been construed as an assault) and exclaimed, 'If it were not assize time, I would not take such language from you'. 'Assize time' meant that the judges were in town and no doubt T feared being arrested and tried. The same principle applies on the facts of this question where Bridges makes a 'qualified' threat to Stevens (answers A and B are therefore incorrect). As a point of interest the older the case law the better law it is, as it has stood the test of time, over 330 years in this case! There can be assault where no force is used, i.e. threats making the other person fear immediate attack, and therefore answer C is incorrect.

Question 12

Answer C — The Police Reform act 2002 s. 46(1) states:

(1) Any person who assaults —
  (a) A designated person in the execution of his duty
  (b) An accredited person in the execution of his duty
  (c) A person assisting a designated or accredited person in the execution of his duty is guilty of an offence

Providing the designated or accredited person was acting in the execution of their duty it is an offence to assault either them or anyone assisting them, therefore answers B and D are incorrect. There is, however, no specific power of arrest therefore answer A is incorrect.

8 Sexual Offences

> **STUDY PREPARATION**
>
> Sexual offences cover a very wide range of activities. In answering these questions there is a real need first of all to identify who is doing what to whom. Usually the key to the offences that arise from such activities is to be found in:
>
> - the ages
> - the attitude and
> - the accompanying circumstances
>
> of the participants.
>
> For some offences consent is the main issue; for others it is the age, sex or number of people involved — or a combination of these factors. Just how far the law should intrude into the latter cases is a matter of some considerable debate — though thankfully not a debate that we intend to rehearse here.
>
> This chapter should be read in conjunction with Chapter 9 which deals with offences against children and other vulnerable people.
>
> Some of the situations created to test your knowledge in this area may seem a little unlikely — but, if you think they're bizarre, you should read the Law Reports!

QUESTIONS

Question 1

FERGUSON met a girl at a party and she agreed to go back to his house. At FERGUSON'S house they consumed a great deal of alcohol and were both drunk. The girl agreed to have sexual intercourse with FERGUSON. However, he was too drunk to have sex. She stated she was not keen any more and went to the bedroom where she fell asleep. Several hours later FERGUSON entered the bedroom and had sex with her whilst she slept.

Has FERGUSON committed rape?
A No, as she had agreed to sex prior to falling asleep.
B No, as her drunkenness was self-induced.
C Yes, even although she agreed earlier.
D Yes, but only if FERGUSON knew that she had changed her mind.

Question 2

JENKINSON is sexually attracted to his male colleague, COLLINS. One night JENKINSON persuades COLLINS to go back to his house, where he thinks he will be able to have sex with him. To ensure sex takes place, JENKINSON plies COLLINS with alcohol, and adds drugs to the drink to stupefy COLLINS. COLLINS becomes all but unconscious. JENKJNSON then has anal sexual intercourse with him.

What offence, if any, has JENKINSON committed?
A Rape.
B Administering drugs for unlawful sexual intercourse.
C Both rape and administering drugs.
D Either rape or administering drugs, but not both.

Question 3

DAWSON, who is female, is lying in the local park one summer's day. Feeling aroused she begins to masturbate herself, openly, and the park is very busy. Several people walk by and see DAWSON. Her vagina is clearly visible, but no one is offended by this behaviour.

Which, if any offence, has she committed?
A Indecent exposure — Vagrancy Act 1824.
B Indecent exposure — Town Police Clauses Act 1847.
C Outraging public decency — common law.
D No offence of indecency has been committed as she is female.

Question 4

CURSON is 15 years of age, but is a mature boy who looks older than he is. He has been infatuated with his neighbour's 25-year-old daughter for some time, and wishes to have sex with her. One night they are alone in CURSON's house and he starts to seduce her. She masturbates CURSON. She fully believes that CURSON is in fact 17 years old; a fact that, albeit mistakenly, her parents have confirmed.

Which of the following is correct?

A The woman has committed a *prima facie* offence of indecent assault, with no defence.
B The woman has committed a *prima facie* offence of indecent assault, but has a defence of mistaken belief.
C The woman has not committed indecent assault as CURSON consented.
D The woman has not committed indecent assault as she has not actually assaulted CURSON.

Question 5

STRUTHERS and his girlfriend, who are both 17 years of age, are in their bedroom. They are joined by STRUTHERS' younger brother who is 13 years of age. Whilst the brother watches, STRUTHERS and his girlfriend participate in mutual masturbation and oral sex.

Is this an act of gross indecency?

A Yes, as they are under 18 and not in private.
B Yes, because the brother is under 14 years of age.
C No, their behaviour does not amount to indecency.
D No, because one of the participants is female.

Question 6

GUNN invites DAVIES who is 19 and suffering from a severe mental handicap back to his house. GUNN then asks DAVIES to take all his clothes off which he willingly does. GUNN then tries to anally penetrate DAVIES, to which DAVIES has freely agreed. GUNN only just manages to penetrate DAVIES, then gives up and sends DAVIES home.

Which of the following is correct?

A GUNN has committed buggery.
B GUNN has committed assault with intent to commit buggery.
C GUNN has committed attempted rape.
D GUNN has committed rape.

Question 7

What is the minimum period for which a sex offender order can be made?
A Three years.
B Four years.
C Five years.
D Six years.

Question 8

STEPHENSON is a convicted sex offender currently on parole. He has been seen by concerned parents every day of the week standing outside a local primary school. He does or says nothing but is always outside the school when the children go home.

In order to apply for a sex offender order, what must be shown?
A An order is necessary to protect the children at the school he is outside from serious harm from STEPHENSON
B An order is necessary to protect the public in general from serious harm from STEPHENSON
C An order is necessary to protect the public, or particular members of the public from serious harm from STEPHENSON
D An order will only be appropriate if STEPHENSON is a convicted child sex offender.

Question 9

The Chief Constable of Northshire Police has applied for a sex offender order against MORRIS. However, the magistrates have decided that there are insufficient grounds to grant such an order. Still concerned that MORRIS will be a danger to the public, the Chief Constable wishes to consider the options available.

Which of the following is correct?
A The Chief Constable can appeal to the Court of Appeal (Criminal Division).
B The Chief Constable can ask for the magistrates to 'state a case'.
C The Chief Constable can appeal to the Court of Appeal (Civil Division).
D The Chief Constable can appeal to the Crown Court.

Question 10

YOUNG lives with his prostitute girlfriend and assists her to attract clients to their flat by placing cards advertising her services in local phone boxes.

In relation to living on immoral earnings contrary to s. 30 of the Sexual Offences Act 1956, what must be proved?

A The prosecution must prove that YOUNG was living on the earnings of a prostitute.
B The prosecution must prove that YOUNG was actively participating in her business as a prostitute.
C YOUNG must prove that he was not living on the earnings of a prostitute.
D YOUNG must prove that he was not actively participating in her business as a prostitute.

Question 11

MARKS and his female secretary HIRST attended a conference in Brussels. While they were there, MARKS tried to get HIRST to have sex with him. She refused and MARKS got angry. He told her that if she didn't have sex with him, he would reduce her wages. MARKS gave HIRST until that night to decide what to do.

In relation to procuring a woman to have sexual intercourse, which of the following is correct?

A As the incident took place outside the UK, the offence is not complete in these circumstances.
B The offence is not complete in these circumstances.
C The offence is not complete in these circumstances, because MARKS has not used physical intimidation.
D The offence will be complete when HIRST agrees to have sexual intercourse with MARKS, as a result of what he said.

Question 12

Two males, both aged 16 years of age, are engaging in an act of buggery in the room of a private bungalow. They have closed the curtains. However, there is a small gap through which a neighbour is watching them.

Is this act of buggery lawful?

A Yes, they have taken all the steps needed to be in private.
B Yes, provided they are not aware they are being watched.
C No, as they are not in private but being watched by a third person.
D No, as they are not over the age of 16 years.

Question 13

PEARD was given a caution for being a common prostitute, and asks you if she can dispute the interpretation of her actions as being 'soliciting'.

Which of the following is correct?
A No, she cannot dispute the caution, as it is not an official caution for an offence.
B No, she cannot dispute the caution as it is only recorded in a police held register.
C Yes, she can apply to a court within 7 days of the caution.
D Yes, she can apply to a court within 14 days of the caution.

Question 14

TURNER has been convicted of possessing indecent photographs of a child. Since being released from prison, having served his sentence, he has changed his home address.

How should this notification of change of address be made?
A It must be made personally at a police station.
B It can be made by sending a written notification to a police station.
C It can be made by sending written notification or by telephoning the police station.
D It must be made by written notification to the Chief Constable.

Question 15

BAKER is a male who wishes to pay a prostitute for sexual intercourse. Having never done this before he is a bit unsure what to do. He gets into his car and drives to a residential area he believes, mistakenly, to be a well-known red light area. He notices a lone female standing near the bus stop; he stops beside her and says, 'Are you doing business?'. Not knowing what he means she says, 'No I'm waiting for a bus; what sort of business are you looking for?'. Confused, BAKER drives straight home.

Which of the following is correct?
A He has committed an offence of kerb-crawling as his behaviour is likely to cause annoyance to the woman.
B He has committed an offence of kerb-crawling as he has solicited the woman from his car.

66 Sexual Offences

C He has not committed an offence of kerb-crawling as the woman was not offended.
D He has not committed an offence of kerb-crawling as he did not intend to cause annoyance to the woman.

Question 16

DAWLISH is a registered sex offender against whom there is an interim sex offenders order. This order prevented DAWLISH from going within 200 metres of any school building. The main application for an order has not yet been determined by the magistrates' court. DAWLISH goes to Scotland on holiday, and is seen by the local Police up there standing immediately outside a school playground, masturbating whilst the children played (this action constitutes a criminal offence in Scotland).

Has DAWLISH committed an offence of breaching a sex offender order?
A Yes, even though he breached the order in Scotland.
B Yes, but only because he was committing a criminal offence in Scotland.
C No, as it was only an interim order only breaches of actual orders apply in Scotland.
D No, breaches only apply to actions in England and Wales.

ANSWERS

Question 1

Answer **C** — This question examines consent, or more importantly in this case, true consent. Rape requires that the intercourse be without the consent of the other party. The question of whether that person consented is one of fact for the jury. There is no requirement that the complainant demonstrates or communicates a lack of consent to the accused. Even where that consent is given, it can be withdrawn at any time (*Kaitamaki* v *The Queen* [1985] AC 147; *R* v *Cooper* [1994] Crim LR 531) and therefore answer A is incorrect. So at the time of penetration was the girl consenting? At the very least FERGUSON was reckless as to whether she was still consenting or not, which is enough to support a conviction for rape (answer D is incorrect). A complainant may well be incapable of consenting due to the influence of drink or drugs, and it would not seem to matter whether she became intoxicated on her own initiative (*R* v *Malone* (1998) 2 Cr App R 447); therefore answer B is incorrect. The answer to this question lies in the case of *R v Mayers* (1872) 12 Cox CC 311, where it was held that a sleeping victim is not deemed to have consented.

Question 2

Answer **A** — Unlike the offence of rape, s. 4(1) of the Sexual Offences Act 1956 is gender specific and states:

> It is an offence for a person to apply or administer to, or cause to be taken by, a *woman* any drug, matter or thing with intent to stupefy or overpower her so as thereby to enable any man to have unlawful sexual intercourse with her.

Answers B and C are therefore incorrect. As stated rape, however, does apply to men and there are precedents relating to consent while not in a position to exercise rational judgement (e.g. while drunk — *R v Lang* (1975) 62 Cr App R 50).

Question 3

Answer **C** — Both the indecent exposure offences can only be committed by males and therefore A and B are incorrect. At common law, it is an indictable offence of outraging public decency to expose the person or to engage in or simulate a sexual act (*R v Mayling* [1963] 3 QB 717). The act must be committed where a real possibility existed that the general public might witness it (*R v Walker* (1996) 1 Cr App R 111). There is nothing at common law to state that males can only commit this offence, so answer D is incorrect.

Question 4

Answer **B** — Where a child is involved there may be an indecent assault even though the victim 'consents' and therefore answer C is incorrect. Indecency is said to be capable of being considered by right-minded persons as indecent (*R v Sargeant* (1997) 161 JP 127), which would include masturbation and therefore answer D is incorrect. The only other factor to consider is that of a defence. In *R v K* [2002] 1 AC 462, the Court of Appeal held that under s. 14(1) of the Sexual Offences Act 1956, a genuine belief by a defendant that a girl was over 16 years of age did not provide a defence of indecent assault on a girl under that age. This has, however, been overturned by the House of Lords who outlined that the prosecution must show the absence of such belief before a conviction can be secured. Curson has a defence; therefore, answer A is incorrect.

Question 5

Answer **D** — The offence of gross indecency can only be committed where a man commits an act of gross indecency with another man, whether in public or private, so answers A, B and C are incorrect. In any case it would not be deemed to be in private as they are being watched by a third party. Whether the behaviour amounts to gross indecency would be a matter for the jury/magistrate to decide. Here as it is a male and female, they cannot commit the offence and the question will never arise.

Question 6

Answer **D** — Buggery can be a lawful, consensual sexual activity. Where there is no such consent, buggery becomes rape. Anyone suffering from a severe mental handicap is unable to give consent to buggery, and GUNN has raped DAVIES. GUNN cannot commit the offence of buggery as buggery is only unlawful where both parties have not achieved the age of 16, or it is not taking place in private, neither of which apply here — answer A is incorrect. It is not attempt rape as rape is described as penetration to the slightest degree — answer C is incorrect. As GUNN has in essence 'performed' buggery, i.e. anal intercourse with DAVIES, he cannot commit an offence of *intention*, i.e. assault with intent to commit buggery — answer B is incorrect. It could be argued that given the vulnerability of the victim this offence was committed prior to actual intercourse, but given the certainty that in law GUNN committed rape this argument becomes irrelevant.

Question 7

Answer **C** — A sex offender order lasts for a minimum of five years and therefore answers A, B and D are incorrect.

Question 8

Answer **C** — The chief officer of police for an area must believe that the person has acted in a way, which *gives reasonable cause to believe* that an order is necessary to protect the public from serious harm from STEPHENSON. The Police Reform Act 2002 has extended the definition of the 'public' for whose protection an order can be sought and made.

In order to apply for a sex offender order, it must:

- Appear to the chief officer that
- The person is a sex offender (not necessary child sex offender, therefore answer D is incorrect)
- To protect the public — or any particular members of the public.

This means that any particular group could be included and not just the public at large; therefore, answer B is incorrect, and also it could be extended to children at all local schools — not just the one he is standing outside of (see *Jones (Peter)* v *Greater Manchester Police Authority* [2002] ACD 4). Therefore, answer A is incorrect.

Question 9

Answer **B** — Where the magistrates' court makes a decision, on the balance of probabilities, against making a sex offender order, there is no right of appeal open to the chief officer; thus, answers A, C and D are incorrect. The chief office could, however, always ask the magistrates to 'state a case' for consideration by the Divisional Court.

Question 10

Answer C — Section 30(2) of the Sexual Offences Act 1956 defines this offence as:

> For the purposes of this section a man who lives with or is habitually in the company of a prostitute, or who exercises control, direction or influence over a prostitute's movements in a way which shows that he is aiding abetting or compelling her prostitution with others, shall be presumed to be knowingly living on the earnings of prostitution, unless he proves the contrary.

All the prosecution has to show is that he is living with a prostitute, so answers A and B are incorrect. The onus is on Young to prove he was not living on the earnings of a prostitute and nothing else and therefore answer D is incorrect.

Question 11

Answer **B** — Section 2 of the Sexual Offences Act 1956 states:

> (1) It is an offence for a person to procure a woman, by threats or intimidation, to have sexual intercourse in any part of the world.

Answer A is therefore incorrect.

As 'procuring' means persuading the woman by whatever means to have sexual intercourse (making answer C incorrect), why is the offence not made out in these circumstances? Simply the act of procurement is not complete until the desired outcome is achieved, i.e. sexual intercourse takes place (*R v Johnson* [1964] 2 QB 404). This makes answer D incorrect.

Question 12

Answer **A** — Buggery is lawful provided that the act of buggery takes place in private and both parties have attained the age of sixteen (answer D is incorrect). Note that this change of age was effected by the Sexual Offences (Amendment) Act 2000 reducing the age from at least 18 to at least 16 years. Section 12(1B) of the Sexual Offences Act 1956 defines private as:

> An act of buggery by one man with another shall not be treated as taking place in private if it takes place — when more than two persons take part or are present . . .

Here there are not more than two persons participating and 'present' would mean present in the room (answer C is incorrect). This is true whether or not they were aware they were being watched.

Question 13

Answer **D** — A woman can dispute the caution by applying to the court within 14 days. Answers A, B and C are therefore incorrect.

Question 14

Answer **B** — There is an option for Turner which does not involve actually attending the station (answer A is incorrect), nor providing written notification to the Chief Constable (answer D is incorrect). The law would be complied with by either attending the station and giving oral notification, or by written notification to the police station. Note the oral notification is only available to those who attend the station, therefore answer C is incorrect.

Question 15

Answer **A** — To prove the offence of kerb-crawling, you have to show *either* the person solicited a woman persistently or in circumstances likely to cause annoyance. As it is not limited to the person's intention answer D is incorrect. Although it can be committed from a motor vehicle, it must meet either of the two tests mentioned (answer B is incorrect). On the subject of persistent soliciting, the prosecution must prove more than one act, i.e. separate approaches to more than one person or two invitations to the same person. In essence, there must be a degree of repetition. We now need to examine annoyance. It is sufficient if there was a *likelihood* of nuisance to other persons in the neighbourhood. In determining that likelihood, the character of the area is taken into account (*Paul* v *DPP* (1989) 90 Cr App R 173). Answer C is incorrect in that, even though the woman propositioned was not insulted, other people may have been; given it is a residential area this is more than likely. Ask yourself this: Would the woman, or any other person in the area, have been annoyed had they known Baker's motives?

Question 16

Answer **A** — The Police Reform Act 2002, *inter alia*, enhanced the existing legislation in relation to sex offenders as outlined in the Crime and Disorder Act 1998. It allows for application of an interim order where the main application has not been determined by the magistrates' court. In essence, however, an interim order's powers mirror an actual order. In particular, ss. 69–71 of the 2002 Act sanction United Kingdom wide powers to enforce sex offenders orders; in particular, making breaches of such orders an offence wherever the offender is. This reciprocal agreement means that breaches of an order determined in England and Wales, including interim orders (which make answer C incorrect), are an offence if the breach is committed in Scotland and *vice versa*. This means that breach is not restricted to actions in England and Wales; therefore, answer D is incorrect. Finally, any action that breaches the order, in this case being within 200 metres of school premises, would be enough. The fact he has committed another offence is irrelevant to the breach; therefore, answer B is incorrect.

9 Offences Against Children and Vulnerable People

> **STUDY PREPARATION**
>
> When all of the provisions of the Youth Justice and Criminal Evidence Act 1999 are finally introduced, the impact on policing is likely to be huge. It is important for all officers to recognise 'vulnerability' amongst witnesses. Many victims of offences contained in this chapter will fall within the definition of a vulnerable witness.
>
> Operational officers deal with situations involving children and vulnerable people on a daily basis; therefore it is important to recognise your powers. On a practical note, many occurrences, such as taking children into police protection under the Children Act 1989, will involve a joint approach with other agencies — use their specialist knowledge in your decision-making processes.
>
> Make sure you know the difference between the two offences under the Child Abduction Act 1984 (person connected to a child and person not connected to a child). These offences have recently been shown to be on the increase. Child cruelty is another important offence to learn, as well as the various sexual offences against children and people suffering from mental impairment.
>
> Custody officers and reviewing officers regularly deal with people detained under s. 136 of the Mental Health Act 1983; therefore, it is important to know when such people may be detained, for how long, and the procedure for dealing with them.

Offences Against Children and Vulnerable People   73

QUESTIONS

Question 1

JUAN was born in Spain, but lives in the UK. He is separated from his wife, GAIL, and their four-year-old son, DAVID. GAIL had custody of DAVID and had refused to let JUAN take DAVID to see his grandparents in Spain. JUAN arranged for his brother to pick up DAVID from school one Friday and take him to Spain. He intended meeting them there, when he finished work later that evening. He knew GAIL would not consent, but intended to return DAVID at the end of the weekend.

In relation to offences that might have been committed under the Child Abduction Act 1984, which of the following is correct?

A   Only JUAN is guilty of an offence; his brother is not 'connected with the child'.
B   Only JUAN's brother is guilty of an offence; he physically took DAVID out of the UK.
C   Both JUAN and his brother are guilty of offences in these circumstances.
D   Neither person is guilty, as they intended to return DAVID to the UK.

Question 2

SHELLEY, aged 18, was a single parent, who had a baby aged 16 months. One winter, the baby developed a severe case of influenza, which resulted in hypothermia. Eventually the baby died. The baby had been ill for some time, and SHELLEY had not taken her to the doctor's. SHELLEY was arrested for the offence of child cruelty, when she reported the death to the police.

What would the prosecution have to prove in order to convict SHELLEY of this offence?

A   That her actions in denying medical care were wilful.
B   That she was reckless in denying medical care for the child.
C   That she intended to deny medical care for the child.
D   That her denying medical care for the child included a positive act.

Question 3

NATHAN, aged 23, worked as a volunteer in a youth club. DANIELLE, aged 15, was a member of the club. DANIELLE told NATHAN that she was 16, and he believed her, as she was in the same class as his sister. One night, when everyone else had left, they had sexual intercourse in his office.

74 Offences Against Children and Vulnerable People

What defence might be available to NATHAN, in answer to a charge under s. 6 of the Sexual Offences Act 1956?

A He has not previously been arrested for an offence under the section.
B He has not previously been convicted of an offence under the section.
C He has not previously been charged with an offence under the section.
D He has not previously been charged with an offence under the Act.

Question 4

CLINTON's cousin, SALLY, has a 15-year-old daughter, KAREN, who looks older than her age. CLINTON introduced KAREN to his friend, GEORGE, who is a pimp. Between them, CLINTON and GEORGE persuaded KAREN to become a prostitute. She agreed and went out with GEORGE on weekends only, and solicited in the street for prostitution. SALLY was not told what was happening to her daughter.

In relation to offences under s. 28 of the Sexual Offences Act 1956 (causing or encouraging prostitution of a girl under 16), which of the following is true?

A GEORGE has committed the offence, but CLINTON has not.
B CLINTON has committed the offence, but GEORGE has not.
C CLINTON and GEORGE have committed the offence in these circumstances.
D Neither person has committed the offence in these circumstances.

Question 5

BELL was drunk and was lying on a bench in a park one afternoon. ALISON, aged 14, and CARRIE, aged 16, were standing nearby. BELL began masturbating. He made no move towards them, but was obviously deriving pleasure from the fact they could see him. The girls were scared and ran away without approaching BELL.

Has BELL committed an offence under s. 1 of the Indecency with Children Act 1960 (indecency with children), in these circumstances?

A Yes, but only in relation to ALISON.
B No, as there was no physical contact.
C Yes, in relation to both girls.
D No, as there was no threat towards the girls.

Question 6

PORTER downloaded some pornographic pictures of children who were under the age of 16 from the Internet. He took them to work the next day, and lent them to his friend, WILLIS, who returned them the next day.

Offences Against Children and Vulnerable People 75

Who, if either, has committed an offence in relation to the photographs?
A Both people: PORTER for possessing and distributing photographs; WILLIS for being in possession of them.
B Only PORTER, for possessing and distributing the photographs to another person.
C Both PORTER and WILLIS for possession, as photographs cannot be 'distributed' to just one person in this way.
D Both PORTER and WILLIS for possession; the offence of 'distributing' does not include lending.

Question 7

Section 46 of the Children Act 1989 deals with the protection of children in certain situations. In relation to that section, which of the following statements is correct?
A A constable or social worker may remove a child to suitable accommodation.
B A constable in uniform may remove a child to suitable accommodation.
C A constable may only remove a child to a police station or hospital.
D A constable may remove a child to suitable accommodation.

Question 8

Constable FENTON attended KHAN's home with a social worker and a doctor. A warrant had been obtained for KHAN's removal to a place of safety under the Mental Health Act 1983. KHAN was detained by Constable FENTON and taken to a police car, but while he was being driven to a police station, KHAN overpowered the officer and escaped.

In relation to a power to retake KHAN, which of the following statements, if any, is correct?
A There is no power to retake him as he was not removed from a public place.
B There is a power to retake him up to 72 hours after his escape.
C There is no power to retake him as he had not arrived at a police station.
D There is a power to retake him up to 72 hours after his arrest.

Question 9

Section 1(2)(b) Children and Young Persons act 1933 outlines that a person will have neglected a child who dies as a result of suffocation (not being suffocation caused by disease or the presence of any foreign body in the throat or air passages of the infant) whilst in bed with that child under the influence of drink.

There are, however, restrictions on age to this offence. What are those restrictions?

A The child must be under 2 and the person over 16.
B The child must be under 3 and the person over 16.
C The child must be under 3 and the person over 18.
D The child must be under 2 and the person over 18.

Question 10

HINDS is a female employed as a cleaner at a hospital specialising in mental health. She is sexually very active and is caught one morning having sexual intercourse with a male patient, who was receiving treatment for a mental disorder at the hospital as an outpatient. Consider only an offence contrary to s. 128 Mental Health Act 1959.

In relation to HINDS' actions, which of the following is correct?

A She has committed this offence, even though the patient is an out-patient.
B She has committed the offence, even though she is not an officer on the staff.
C She has not committed the offence, because she is not an officer on the staff.
D She has not committed the offence because she is a woman.

ANSWERS

Question 1

Answer **C** — There are two offences under the Child Abduction Act 1984 that deal with taking a child under the age of 16.

Under s. 1 of the Act, an offence takes place where a person connected with a child under the age of 16 takes or sends the child out of the UK without the appropriate consent. This offence *may only be committed by a 'connected person'*; who will include the child's parent, father even if the parents are not married, the legal guardian, or a person with a residence order or lawful custody order.

As Juan's brother does not fall within this group, he cannot commit this offence. However, to lawfully take David out of the UK, Juan would require the consent of the mother/guardian/person with a residence order or person with custody.

Obviously Juan did not have consent to take David out of the UK, and even though he did not actually take him, he committed the offence by sending him. Sending can

Offences Against Children and Vulnerable People **77**

include 'causing', or 'inducing', a child to go with another, which is why answer B is incorrect.

Under s. 2 of the Act, a person commits an offence if, without lawful authority or reasonable excuse, he takes or detains a child under the age of 16 so as to remove him from the lawful control of any person having lawful control of the child; or so as to keep him out of the lawful control of any person entitled to lawful control of the child (which would include Gail). This offence may be committed by a person *who is not a 'connected person'*, and would be committed by the brother (which is why answer A is incorrect).

There is no requirement for the abduction to be permanent (making answer D incorrect).

Question 2

Answer **A** — The circumstances in the question may amount to neglect, but the prosecution must prove that this was *wilful* (not reckless or intentional, which is why answers B and C are incorrect). The issue of *mens rea* was addressed in the case of *R* v *Sheppard* [1981] AC 394. Lord Diplock explained that:

> . . . the jury must be satisfied (1) that the child did in fact need medical aid at the time at which the parent is charged with failing to provide it (the *actus reus*) and (2) either that the parent was aware at the time that the child's health might be at risk if it were not provided with medical aid, or that the parent's unawareness of this fact was due to his not caring whether the child's health was at risk or not (the *mens rea*).

There may be an element of 'objective recklessness' in the defendant's behaviour. However, the definition requires proof that a person was wilful in their actions.

Answer D is incorrect, as the offence can be committed either by an act *or* by an omission.

Question 3

Answer **C** — Section 6 of the Sexual Offences Act 1956 makes it an offence for a man to have unlawful sexual intercourse with a girl under the age of 16. Under s. 1(3), a man is not guilty of an offence under s. 6 if he is under the age of 24 and has not previously been *charged with a like offence*, and he believes her to be of the age of 16 or over and has reasonable cause for that belief.

'A like offence' means an offence under *this section* or an attempt to commit one. Answers A, B and D are therefore incorrect.

Question 4

Answer **D** — This offence is not limited to prostitution, but also includes the condoning of an indecent assault. It *only* applies to people who 'are responsible' for girls under 16, which will include parents, guardians and anyone into whose charge a child has been given.

Neither person in the scenario has any degree of parental control over the girl and therefore they cannot commit the offence (answers A, B and C are incorrect). The mother was unaware of the situation, and is unlikely to have any criminal liability under this offence.

It is likely that the persons in the scenario will have committed other offences under the Act, such as controlling movements of prostitutes and living from immoral earnings.

Question 5

Answer **A** — The offence is committed where a person commits an act of gross indecency with or towards a child under the age of 16, or who incites a child under that age to such an act with him or another. (Answer C is therefore incorrect as only one of the girls was under 16.)

There is no requirement for physical contact, and in the case of *R v Francis* (1988) 88 Cr App R 127, it was decided that masturbating in the presence of children can amount to an offence, provided the defendant knows that the children are aware of what is going on (it would not be so straightforward if he were hiding in a bush). The act must be in some way directed towards the children, at the very least, by the accused deriving satisfaction from the knowledge that the children were watching what he is doing. (Answer B is therefore incorrect.)

Answer D is incorrect because the offence can be committed where the defendant is passive. Contrast this with the offence of indecent assault, where there must be some 'hostile act', in order to complete the offence.

Question 6

Answer **A** — There are two offences here. The first offence is under the Protection of Children Act 1978, of taking, making, distributing, showing, publishing, advertising and possessing with intent to distribute indecent photographs.

The second offence is committed under the Criminal Justice Act 1988, which added the offence of mere possession of such photography.

Therefore, offences would be committed in the scenario by the person distributing

(PORTER), and the people possessing (both PORTER and WILLIS), and therefore answer B is incorrect.

The offence of distribution is to 'another person'. There is no requirement to distribute to more than one person; therefore, answer C is incorrect.

Distributing *will* include lending, which is why answer D is incorrect.

Question 7

Answer **D** — Section 46 of the Children Act 1989 states that where a *constable* has reasonable cause to believe that a child would otherwise be likely to suffer significant harm, he or she may remove that child to *suitable accommodation* and keep him or her there.

Answer A is incorrect, as the section only allows a constable to remove the child (known as police protection). There is no requirement for the officer to be in uniform and therefore answer B is incorrect.

The section does not specify that the child should *only* be taken to a police station or hospital (although these may be suitable places), the child may be taken to any *suitable accommodation* (which is why answer C is incorrect).

Question 8

Answer **B** — Under s. 138(3) of the Mental Health Act 1983, a person who has been removed under s. 136 (public place) or under a warrant, who subsequently escapes while being taken to or while being detained at a place of safety, *cannot be retaken after 72 hours elapses*. This means that they *can* be re-taken during the 72-hour period.

The time period is calculated as follows. If a person escapes *before* they reach a place of safety, the 72 hours is taken from the time of escape (answers C and D are therefore incorrect). If a person escapes *after arriving* at a place of safety, the 72 hours begins from the time they arrived at that place.

Answer A is incorrect, as a person may be taken under warrant, as well as from a public place, under this Act.

Question 9

Answer **B** — Children and Young Persons Act 1933, s. 1 (2) states:

> (b) where it is proved that the death of an infant under three years of age was caused by suffocation (not being suffocation caused by disease or the presence of any foreign body in the throat or air passages of the infant) while the infant was in

80 Offences Against Children and Vulnerable People

> bed with some other person who has attained the age of sixteen years, that other person shall, if he was, when he went to bed, under the influence of drink, be deemed to have neglected the infant in a manner likely to cause injury to its health.

The child must be under 3 years of age, and like other aspects of this offence the person must be at least 16 years of age, answers A, C and D are therefore incorrect.

Question 10

Answer **D** — s. 128 Mental Health Act 1959 (Sexual intercourse with patients) states:

(1) *Without prejudice to s. 7 of the Sexual Offences Act 1956, it shall be an offence, subject to the exception mentioned in this section —*
   (a) *for a man who is an officer on the staff of or is otherwise employed in, or is one of the managers of, a hospital or mental nursing home to have unlawful sexual intercourse with a woman who is for the time being receiving treatment for mental disorder in that hospital or home, or to have such intercourse on the premises of which the hospital or home forms part, with a woman who is for the time being receiving such treatment there as an out-patient;*

As it includes persons who are employed by the hospital, HINDS would be included; therefore, answer C is incorrect. However, as it clearly states that the offence can only be committed by a man, HINDS cannot commit this offence; therefore, answers A and B are incorrect. Note also the fact that although the patient was only an outpatient, they could still fall victim to this offence.

10 Offences Amounting to Dishonesty, Deception and Fraud

STUDY PREPARATION

To use the police vernacular, many subjects in this chapter are your 'bread and butter' offences. In the *Police Q & As Road Traffic* book, we stress the importance of knowing basic definitions, in order to recognise the more complex offences. The same applies to many dishonesty offences. You simply cannot get away with not knowing the components that make up the definition of theft. Learning this will assist you with robbery, handling, burglary and aggravated burglary. Similarly, the concept of dishonesty is important to understanding — and proving — a number of offences.

Following on from this, you must be able to recognise the difference between the burglary offences under s. 9(1)(a) and s. 9(1)(b) of the Theft Act 1968, and when a person commits the aggravated offence, by having with them certain articles. Learning the definitions of robbery and handling will also be crucial, as well as the offences under s. 12 of the Act (taking and aggravated vehicle-taking).

There are other offences contained in the chapter that you may not come across regularly, such as abstracting electricity and blackmail. Deception offences are also important.

There is often an overlap between the various offences of deception; it is important to recognise the differences between each one. Practically, police officers are more likely to encounter deception where it arises from people obtaining property and services, as well as making off without payment. However, for completeness it is important to know all the offences, such as fraud, forgery, obtaining pecuniary advantage and evading liability.

QUESTIONS

Question 1

HARDING was in a shop with PERRY, who picked up a CD, intending to steal it. PERRY realised he was being watched by SATO, a store detective, and placed it in HARDING'S pocket, without HARDING knowing. Before they left the store, HARDING realised what PERRY had done, and was about to put the CD back, but changed his mind and decided to keep it and try to leave without paying. On their way out, SATO stopped them.

Has HARDING committed an offence in these circumstances?
A No, as PERRY was the one who appropriated the property.
B Yes, he has committed the offence of theft in these circumstances.
C No, as he formed the intent to steal after appropriating the property.
D Yes, he has committed the offence of handling in these circumstances.

Question 2

PREECE was out walking in a meadow near her home, when she decided to pick a bunch of wildflowers to create a flower display for her dining room.

Which of the following statements is correct in relation to 'property' as defined by s. 4 of the Theft Act 1968?
A The flowers are wild and are therefore not 'property'.
B Only flowers grown commercially are 'property'.
C 'Wild' relates only to mushrooms, not flowers or foliage.
D Wildflowers become property only if picked for some reward.

Question 3

HARVEY was walking past a post office, when he saw an elderly woman coming out. HARVEY produced a knife and threatened her, demanding she handed over her handbag. He had no intention of using the knife, but was trying to make the woman hand over her handbag. The woman was not scared and began hitting him with her bag until he eventually ran away.

Has HARVEY committed the offence of robbery in these circumstances?
A No, as the person was not put in fear of violence being used against her.
B Yes, as he intended to put her in fear of violence being used against her.

C No, but he could have committed attempted robbery.
D Yes, as he has committed attempted theft, using violence.

Question 4

LEWIS has had a dispute with his neighbour, PLATT. One night LEWIS got home from the pub having had too much to drink and found paint had been poured over his car. He was convinced that PLATT was responsible and so forced his way into PLATT'S house. LEWIS intended to beat PLATT up, causing really serious injury; however, he discovered the house was empty.

> In relation to the offence of burglary (under s. 9 of the Theft Act 1968), which of the following is correct?

A An offence under s. 9(1)(b) has been committed even though no grievous bodily harm was caused.
B An offence under s. 9(1)(a) has not been committed as no grievous bodily harm was caused.
C An offence under s. 9(1)(a) has been committed even though no grievous bodily harm was caused.
D An offence under s. 9(1)(a) has not been committed as no assault or theft was carried out.

Question 5

PAUL and his family sold their house and bought a large camper van, which they kept permanently on a campsite. While they were out, MORRIS, tired from hitchhiking, broke the door lock to sleep inside the van. Having fallen asleep on a bunk bed, MORRIS was woken up by the sound of children. He ran from the van grabbing some cans of food on the way out.

> Which of the following is correct in relation to MORRIS?

A He has *not* committed burglary as a camper van is a vehicle, never a 'building'.
B He has committed burglary, under s. 9(1)(b), as a camper van is a 'building' here.
C He has committed burglary, under s. 9(1)(a), as a camper van is a 'building' here.
D He has *not* committed burglary, as the camper van was not occupied when he entered.

Question 6

GORDON broke into CRAWFORD's house one day, intending to steal property. Unknown to him, she was asleep in bed, having worked nights. GORDON entered the bedroom and when he saw her on the bed, he decided to force her to have sex with him. He took off his belt and tied her hands together and while she struggled, he raped her. He left the house without stealing anything and CRAWFORD suffered no serious physical injuries.

> Has GORDON committed the offence of aggravated burglary, under s. 10 of the Theft Act 1968?
>
> A Yes, from the time he intended to use his belt.
> B No, he has not committed the offence.
> C Yes, from the time he tied CRAWFORD up.
> D Yes, from the time he entered the house.

Question 7

PARSONS asked his colleague JAMES if he could borrow her motor van to take his family on holiday for the weekend to West Wales. JAMES agreed, however, PARSONS had misled JAMES, and actually took the motor van to a pop festival with some friends. He returned it in good condition at the end of the weekend.

> Has PARSONS committed an offence (under s. 12 of the Theft Act 1968) of taking a vehicle without the owner's consent?
>
> A Yes, he obtained JAMES' permission by deception.
> B Yes, but only if the journey was further than the agreed destination.
> C No, his deception did not negate the consent he obtained.
> D Yes, unless he could show he believed JAMES would have consented.

Question 8

WEBB and LARTER were in a supermarket car park when they saw a car with the keys in the ignition. They decided to take the vehicle and WEBB got in the driver's seat, and LARTER sat in the front passenger seat. While he was reversing out of the parking place, WEBB struck KANG, a shopper who was walking past. Both people got out of the car and ran off, leaving KANG behind with a bruised hip.

> Has an offence been committed (under s. 12A of the Theft Act 1968) of aggravated vehicle-taking?
>
> A No, the vehicle was not driven on a road.
> B Yes, but only by WEBB, the driver.
> C Only if it can be shown that the vehicle was driven dangerously.
> D Yes, by both WEBB and LARTER.

Question 9

HOWELLS was working for a company that was going through financial difficulties, and as a result, he was laid off. One Friday evening, HOWELLS entered the company office through an insecure window. In order to cause financial hardship to the owners, he linked all the computers up to the Internet, intending that they should all stay on for the weekend.

Has HOWELLS committed the offence of abstracting electricity by his actions?
A Yes, the offence is complete in these circumstances.
B Yes, but a charge of burglary would be more appropriate.
C No, because he has not abstracted or diverted electricity.
D No, using a telephone would not amount to using electricity.

Question 10

TAYLOR and RUSSELL met one evening to discuss breaking into an electrical warehouse. It was agreed that TAYLOR would break in and hand the goods to RUSSELL outside in his van. They were joined by BIRCH, who agreed to keep the goods in his house for a few weeks, and MURPHY, who owned a second-hand store, and would sell the goods. They agreed that the burglary would take place the following night.

Who, if any, has committed the offence of handling stolen goods in these circumstances?
A RUSSELL, BIRCH and MURPHY only.
B All four have committed the offence.
C Only BIRCH and MURPHY have committed the offence.
D None of these people have committed the offence.

Question 11

Which of the following statements is/are correct in relation to the offence of handling?
1. A person cannot be convicted of handling if the goods were stolen outside England and Wales.
2. Goods obtained by deception and blackmail are included in the definition of handling.

A Statement 1 only.
B Statement 2 only.
C Both statements 1 and 2.
D Neither statement.

Question 12

VINCENT applied for a job with a computer company. He falsely stated in his application form that he was proficient in using several computer packages, which were required by the company in the job description that was sent out with the application form. He was later interviewed, but was unsuccessful and did not get the job.

Has VINCENT committed an offence (under s. 16 of the Theft Act 1968) of obtaining a pecuniary advantage in these circumstances?

A Yes, even though he has not profited from his actions.
B No, because he has not made a financial gain.
C No, he has not received the opportunity to earn remuneration.
D Yes, he deceived the company into interviewing him.

Question 13

FRENCH and OSBORN went for a meal in their favourite restaurant, where they ate regularly. During the meal, they consumed two bottles of wine each, and for a laugh, at the end of the meal they both went to the toilet and climbed out of the window. They intended returning the next day to pay for the meal; however, the restaurant owner did not know and called the police.

Have FRENCH AND OSBORN committed an offence (under s. 3 of the Theft Act 1978) of making off without payment?

A Yes, but they would have a defence if they could show that they thought the owner would have consented in the circumstances.
B No, because they have not deceived the owner into thinking they would pay for the meals.
C No, they have not committed the offence in these circumstances as they intended returning to pay.
D Yes, they have committed the offence, regardless of their intention to pay, and would have no defence in the circumstances.

Question 14

GOMEZ was at his friend PETERS' flat and he had with him a stolen credit card, which he had recently used to obtain goods by deception. GOMEZ gave the card to PETERS, so that he could use it the next day. GOMEZ had no intention of using the card again.

Which of the following statements is true, in relation to s. 25 of the Theft Act 1968, regarding 'going equipped'?

A An offence has been committed by PETERS only, as GOMEZ did not intend using the card again.
B An offence has been committed by GOMEZ and PETERS in these circumstances.
C No offence has been committed by either PETERS or GOMEZ, as they were both in a dwelling.
D An offence has been committed by GOMEZ; PETERS commits no offence in these circumstances.

Question 15

GORDON fancied CLINTON, who worked with him. He asked her out during a Christmas party, but she refused, as she was married. The following day, GORDON sent CLINTON an e-mail, stating that, unless she had sex with him, he was going to phone her husband and tell him they were having an affair.

Has GORDON committed the offence of blackmail in these circumstances?
A Yes, if it can be shown that CLINTON was in fear of the consequences.
B No, as GORDON was not seeking to gain or cause loss.
C Yes, as GORDON has made unwarranted demands with menace.
D No, the offence is only committed where a person demands money or other property.

Question 16

SCOTT was homeless and was sitting on a bench in the centre of his local town. He was sitting next to a bucket which had 'SAVE THE CHILDREN' written on it. Believing he was collecting money for charity, several people placed money in the bucket. SCOTT, who was trying to get money for food and not for charity, did not say anything at any time.

Has SCOTT committed an offence (under s. 15 of the Theft Act 1968) of obtaining property by deception?
A No, it cannot be shown that he used words to obtain property by deception.
B Yes, but only if it can be proved that he intended people to be deceived.
C Yes, but only if it can be shown that he was reckless as to whether people were deceived.
D No, he did not use any words or actions to obtain property by change deception.

Question 17

GRANT is a member of a gym to which she took DUNCAN. At the gym there was a new person working in reception and GRANT showed her membership card to the receptionist, saying, 'She's a member, too, but she forgot her card'. DUNCAN was not a member, but said nothing and was allowed entry, without paying the usual fee for guests.

Who, if any one, has committed an offence (under s. 1 of the Theft Act 1978) of obtaining a service by deception?

A Both have committed the offence in these circumstances.
B DUNCAN only; there is no offence of obtaining a service for another.
C Neither; the offence applies to a service that will be paid for in the future.
D Neither; they have committed the offence of evasion of liability s. 2(1)(c) Theft Act.

Question 18

GORDON ordered some furniture from a second-hand shop. He paid a deposit and was due to pay the remainder on delivery. When the furniture arrived, GORDON gave the delivery driver a cheque, aware that it would not be honoured by the bank. However, he knew that he would have money in the relevant account in a month's time, and would be able to pay the bill then.

Has GORDON committed an offence (under s. 2(1)(b) of the Theft Act 1978) of evasion of liability by deception?

A Yes, but only if the shop owner decides to forgo the payment.
B No, as he does not intend to make a permanent default on the payment.
C Yes, he has made the shop owner wait for the money, which is an offence.
D No, the cheque represents payment, even if later it is not honoured.

Question 19

In relation to the intent required for an offence (under s. 17 of the Theft Act 1968) of false accounting, which of the following statements is correct?
1. The defendant's actions must be accompanied by an intention to permanently deprive.
2. The defendant's actions must take place with a view to gain for them and to cause loss to another.

A Both statements.
B Statement 1 only.
C Neither statement.
D Statement 2 only.

Question 20

CHANDLER is highly skilled in the forgery field, and produced a sophisticated set of plates, from which he made a forged £20 note. Using a high specification laser copier, he photocopied a large quantity of these notes. Before releasing the notes, he spent some in local shops to test their quality.

> Which elements of 'false instrument' would CHANDLER be guilty of in these circumstances?
>
> A Making and using a false instrument.
> B Copying and making a false instrument.
> C Using a false instrument only.
> D He is not guilty of any false instrument offence.

Question 21

GRAINGER is standing by a bus stop when his friend CARTER arrives in a motor vehicle and offers him a lift. Whilst the vehicle was stationary, and switched off, GRAINGER notices that the ignition barrel of the vehicle has been damaged and suspects that the vehicle has been stolen. GRAINGER asks CARTER if the vehicle is stolen and CARTER says, 'what do you think?'. GRAINGER is still unsure if the vehicle is stolen or not. CARTER goes to start the engine but police officers arrive and arrest both GRAINGER and CARTER as the vehicle was taken without consent, although this was not by CARTER.

> Has GRAINGER committed the offence under Theft Act 1968, s. 12(1) of allowing himself to be carried?
>
> A Yes, the fact he suspects the car to be stolen and his presence in it is enough movement of the car is irrelevant.
> B Yes, as the vehicle was actually taken without consent and GRAINGER suspects it was.
> C No, as the vehicle did not actually move he cannot commit this offence; movement is essential.
> D No, mere suspicion is not enough, GRAINGER must know the car is stolen; movement of the car is irrelevant.

Question 22

MILLIGAN commits a robbery and steals a mobile phone. He gives it to COMMONS, who works for a mobile telephone company, who alters the unique device identifier and sells the phone on to an unsuspecting buyer.

Considering The Mobile Telephones (Re-Programming) Act 2002, which of the following is true?

A This is an offence from the moment the phone is altered, there is no defence.
B This is an offence from the moment the phone is sold, there is no defence.
C This is an offence from the moment the phone is altered, there is a statutory defence however.
D This is an offence from the moment the phone is sold there is a statutory defence however.

Question 23

KAPARSKI applies for a mortgage from a leading building society, who provide a free mortgage service. He falsely claims that he has a job and that he earns £20,000 per year. He provides accounts and testimonials, which are false to obtain the mortgage. KAPARSKI hopes to be able to pay the monthly repayments, but this is unlikely given his unemployed status. The building society gives him the loan; however, they would not have done so if it had not been for his practised deception.

Which of the following is correct?

A KAPARSKI has obtained property by deception, as he deceived the building society.
B KAPARSKI has not committed any deception offence, there is no intention to permanently deprive.
C KAPARSKI has not obtained services by deception, as the mortgage service is provided free.
D KAPARSKI has committed an offence of obtaining services by deception.

ANSWERS

Question 1

Answer **B** — A person commits theft if he or she dishonestly appropriates property belonging to another with the intention of permanently depriving the other of it (s. 1 of the Theft Act 1968).

Both people have 'appropriated' property in these circumstances, even though Harding did so after he realised the property was in his pocket (therefore answer A is incorrect). Under s. 3(1), if having come by property (innocently or not) a person later assumes the rights of the owner, he or she commits theft (which is why answer C is incorrect). It is of no relevance that Harding initially decided to return the property.

As the offence of handling will not be committed during the course of a theft, answer D is incorrect.

Question 2

Answer **D** — Under s. 4(3) of the Theft Act 1968, a person who picks mushrooms growing wild on any land, or who picks flowers, fruit or foliage from a plant growing wild on any land, does not (although not in possession of the land) steal what he or she picks, *unless he or she does it for reward or for sale or other commercial purpose.* For purposes of this subsection, 'mushroom' includes any fungus, and 'plant' includes any shrub or tree. Consequently, answers A, B and C are incorrect.

Question 3

Answer **C** — To commit robbery, a person must steal and immediately before or at the time of doing so and in order to do so use force on any person or put **or seek to put** a person in fear of being subjected to force then and there.

B is incorrect, as HARVEY did not steal anything; therefore, he has not committed the full offence of robbery. He would be guilty of attempted robbery in these circumstances, as he sought to put the person in fear of being subjected to force (even though she was not actually scared — making **A** wrong). Further, whether or not he intended to use force is not relevant; his intent that the person should fear that he would is what counts in these circumstances, and finally the full offence of theft **must** take place. Therefore, answer D is incorrect.

Question 4

Answer **C** — A person who enters a building as a trespasser *with intent to inflict* grievous bodily harm commits an offence under s. 9(1)(a) of the Theft Act 1968 (therefore answer B is incorrect). In proving an intention to commit grievous bodily harm under s. 9(1)(a), it is not necessary to prove that an assault was actually committed (*Metropolitan Police Commissioner* v *Wilson* [1984] AC 242) and thus answer D is incorrect.

An offence was not committed under s. 9(1)(b), as a person must be shown to have inflicted grievous bodily harm under that section (answer A is therefore incorrect).

Question 5

Answer **B** — Something will qualify as a 'building' if it has some degree of permanence. In *B* v *Leathley* [1979] Crim LR 314, the Crown Court held that the defendants had committed burglary. They had stolen some meat from a freezer container in a farmyard, which was considered to be permanently in place.

The meaning of 'building' is extended by s. 9(3), and includes an inhabited vehicle or vessel, and applies to any such vehicle or vessel at times when the person having a habitation in it is *not in residence as well as at times when he or she is*. (This makes both answers A and D incorrect.)

Answer C is incorrect because of the intention of the person when he entered the building. Morris entered intending to sleep (not one of the pre-requisites of s. 9(1)(a)). Morris did, however, steal property, having entered as a trespasser, which makes him guilty of burglary under s. 9(1)(b).

Question 6

Answer **B** — A person is guilty of aggravated burglary if he commits burglary and at the time he has with him any firearm, imitation firearm, weapon of offence or explosive.

The person must have the weapon with them *at the time* of committing the offence — in other words, *at the point of entry* for s. 9(1)(a) or *at the time of inflicting grievous bodily harm or committing theft* for s. 9(1)(b).

Applying the Theft Act 1968 to the given circumstances, Gordon committed burglary under s. 9(1)(a) when he entered the house intending to steal. At that time he had his belt with him, but at that time, his belt could not be construed as a weapon of offence — which is defined as 'any article made or adapted for use for causing injury to or incapacitating a person, or intended by the person for such use'. The belt was not made for incapacitating a person and was not intended/adapted to do so when he entered the house (which is why answer D is incorrect).

When Gordon decided to use his belt, he formed the required intent in relation to a weapon of offence (answer A), and when he used it, he adapted it (answer C). However, he did not commit burglary contrary to s. 9(1)(b), as he did not steal or inflict grievous bodily harm at any time.

Quite obviously, Gordon has committed the offence of rape in these circumstances.

Question 7

Answer C — An offence under s. 12 is committed by a person who takes a vehicle without the owner's consent or other lawful authority, for his own or another's use.

The issue of consent was dealt with in the case of *R v Peart* [1970] 2 QB 672. The defendant was convicted of the offence, after he falsely represented to the owner of a car that he needed it to drive from Bedlington to Alnwick to sign a contract. The owner let him have the vehicle, provided he returned it that day. As he had intended all along, Peart drove the car instead to Burnley in the evening.

The Court of Appeal subsequently quashed Peart's conviction, by following the decision in *Whittaker v Campbell* [1984] QB 318, where it was held that *there is no general principle of law that fraud vitiates consent.*

Consequently, even if consent is obtained by fraud, it is still consent (making answer A incorrect). The case of *Peart* shows that even though the journey taken was different from the one agreed, an offence is still not committed (making answer B incorrect).

Finally, the defence provided under s. 12(6) would apply *where an offence has been committed*. Since an offence has not been committed in these circumstances, the defence would not apply (which is why answer D is incorrect).

Question 8

Answer D — First, a person must commit an offence under s. 12(1), of the Theft Act 1968 either by taking the vehicle *or* being carried in it. Then, under s. 12A, it must be proved that any time after the vehicle was taken (whether by him or another), and before it was recovered, that:

- it was driven dangerously on a road or public place; or
- owing to the driving of the vehicle, an accident occurred whereby injury was caused to any person; or
- owing to the driving of the vehicle, an accident occurred whereby damage was caused to any property other than the vehicle; or
- damage was caused to the vehicle.

The Act does not specify that the accident involving an injury to a person should occur on a road (making answer A incorrect).

All that the prosecution has to prove is that *one* of the circumstances above occurred before the car was recovered (*Dawes v DPP* (1995) 1 Cr App R 65) (answer C is incorrect for this reason).

Answer A is incorrect because the offence may be committed by either the driver or the passenger, provided one of the circumstances apply.

Question 9

Answer **A** — Under s. 13 of the Theft Act 1968, a person who dishonestly uses without due authority, or dishonestly causes to be *wasted or diverted*, any electricity shall be guilty of an offence.

As electricity is not 'property', a specific offence was created to deal with its dishonest use or waste. For this reason electricity cannot be 'stolen' and therefore its dishonest use or wastage cannot form an element of burglary (making answer B incorrect).

Diverting a domestic electrical supply so as to bypass the meter or using another's telephone without authority (*Low* v *Blease* [1975] Crim LR 513) would be examples of this offence, as would unauthorised surfing on the Internet by an employee at work, provided in each case that dishonesty was present (making answers C and D incorrect).

Question 10

Answer **D** — Quite simply, there can be no offence under s. 26 of the Theft Act 1968, unless goods have been stolen (answers A and B are therefore incorrect). Even though two of the participants have arranged to receive stolen goods, they will not commit the offence until the burglary takes place (answer C is therefore also incorrect).

If the plan ever does come to fruition, Taylor, as the person stealing the goods, would not commit the offence. It is debatable whether Russell would do so, if he assisted with the burglary, as he might be guilty of that offence.

Question 11

Answer **B** — A person *can* be convicted of handling, if the goods were stolen outside England and Wales, *but* only if the goods were taken under circumstances which amounted to an offence in the other country (answers A and C are therefore incorrect).

Goods obtained by deception and blackmail *are* included in the definition of handling, which makes statement 2 correct and answer D incorrect.

Question 12

Answer **C** — A person who by any deception dishonestly obtains for himself any pecuniary advantage commits an offence. A pecuniary advantage may be obtained either when trying to borrow from an overdraft, taking out a policy of insurance or when given the opportunity to earn remuneration or greater remuneration in employment (or betting).

In the circumstances given, Vincent has not obtained the opportunity to earn remuneration, as he was not been given the job. (Although an attempt to commit the offence may be present, answer D is therefore incorrect.)

There is no requirement for a person to actually profit from their deception; therefore, if he had been successful with his application, answer A would have been correct. Answer B is incorrect in any circumstances.

Question 13

Answer C — This is a typical question where police officers would think practically and think, 'I would arrest those' (now arrestable offence). Avoid this approach and answer questions purely as points of law.

A person commits an offence under s. 3 of the Theft Act 1978 if, knowing that payment on the spot for goods supplied or services received is required, they dishonestly make off without paying *with intent to avoid payment*.

In the scenario, even though the couple have made off without paying, there is no offence if they intend to defer payment to a later date (even though morally their actions may be regarded as wrong!) (Answer D is therefore incorrect).

There is no requirement that the person practised some deception to prove the offence; simply making off with the required intent is enough (which is why answer B is incorrect).

The defence in answer A has been made up and does not exist.

Question 14

Answer **D** — A person commits an offence under s. 25 of the Theft Act 1968 when, not at his place of abode, he has with him any article for use in the course of or in connection with any burglary, theft or cheat (cheat includes deception).

The offence is designed as a preventative measure and therefore cannot be committed by a deed done in the past. The offence will be committed by a person who has an article with them for use by *someone else* (*R v Ellames* [1974] 3 All ER 130).

Applying the Act to this scenario, Gomez was not at his place of abode and had with him a credit card, which he intended Peters to use in the future in a cheat (offence committed, even though he had no intention of using it again, which is why answer A is incorrect).

The card was given to Peters and although he intended using it, he *was* at his place of abode. Consequently, no offence is committed until Peters leaves his house and therefore answer B is incorrect.

Answer C is incorrect because the offence may be committed by a person in a dwelling — provided it is not the place where they live!

Question 15

Answer B — Blackmail is committed when a person, with a view to gain for himself or another or with intent to cause loss to another, makes any unwarranted demands with menaces, (s. 21 of the Theft Act 1968).

Under s. 34 of the Act, 'gain' and 'loss' mean to gain or lose in money or other property. It will not apply where a person is making demands for sexual favours. Consequently, answers A, C and D are incorrect.

Question 16

Answer C — The prosecution would have to show that Scott either intended people to believe he was collecting money for charity *or* that he was reckless to that fact (making B incorrect). The reckless element is subjective, although the prosecution would have to show that the defendant at least gave some thought to his conduct (*R v Goldman* [1997] Crim LR 894).

Conduct can include *omissions*, (*R v Shama* [1990] 1 WLR 661); therefore, the fact that the person did not say or do anything would not provide a defence (which is why answers A and D are incorrect).

Question 17

Answer A — A deception occurs where a person has induced another to confer a benefit by doing some act, or causing or permitting some act to be done, on the understanding that a benefit *has been or will* be paid for (therefore answer C is incorrect).

The Court of Appeal has accepted that obtaining a service for another will amount to an offence under s. 1 of the Theft Act 1978 (*R v Nathan* [1997] Crim LR 835), making answer B incorrect.

Evasion of liability is dealt with later in the chapter, but the circumstances outlined do not constitute an offence under s. 2(1)(c), as there is no provision under the section in respect of obtaining an abatement of liability *for another* (therefore answer D is incorrect).

Question 18

Answer B — A person commits an offence under s. 2(1)(b) of the Theft Act 1978 if, with intent to make *permanent default* in whole or in part on any existing liability to make a payment, or with intent to let another do so, he or she dishonestly induces the creditor or any person claiming payment on behalf of the creditor to wait for payment (whether or not the due date for payment is deferred) or to forgo payment.

Even though he has made the shop owner wait for the money, it would have to be shown that Gordon intended to *permanently* default on the payment (for example, if Gordon moved address after presenting the cheque), which is why answer C is incorrect.

Unlike the other two offences in s. 2(1), it is not necessary under s. 2(1)(b) to show that the person to whom the money was owed decided to forgo all or part of the payment (making answer A incorrect).

Answer D is incorrect because s. 2(3) of the Act, states:

> For purposes of subsection (1)(b) a person induced to take in payment a cheque or other security for money by way of conditional satisfaction of a pre-existing liability is to be treated *not* as being paid but as being induced to wait for payment.

Question 19

Answer **C** — Under s. 17 of the Theft Act 1968, a person must act dishonestly with a view to gain for himself or another *or* (not and), with intent to cause loss to another.

The offence is complete when a person destroys, defaces, conceals or falsifies any account or any record or document made or required for any accounting purpose; or in furnishing information for any purpose produces or makes use of any account, or any such record or document as aforesaid, which to his knowledge is or may be misleading, false or deceptive in a material particular.

Unlike theft, there is no requirement to prove an intention permanently to deprive but there is a need to show dishonesty.

Therefore, *both* statements are incorrect and answers A, B and D are consequently incorrect.

Question 20

Answer **D** — Quite simply, offences classed as forgery include virtually every kind of document *except* bank notes. Therefore, as he has been involved in 'forging' bank notes, Chandler cannot commit the offences of making and using a false instrument (answer A is incorrect), copying and making a false instrument (answer B is incorrect) and using a false instrument (answer C is incorrect). Offences relating to currency are dealt with by the Forgery and Counterfeiting Act 1981.

Question 21

Answer C — On a charge of driving or allowing himself to be carried in or on a conveyance taken without authority, it must be proved that the accused knew that the conveyance had been taken without lawful authority (*R v Diggin* (1980) 72 Cr App R 204, *Boldizsar v Knight* [1980] Crim LR 653); therefore, answers A and B are incorrect. However, it seems that the accused need not be aware that the taker took the conveyance for his own or another's use.

It is also not enough for the prosecution to prove that the accused was in or on the conveyance. There must have been some movement of the conveyance (*R v Miller* [1976] Crim LR 417; also see *Diggin*). If a taker of a motor vehicle offers a person a lift and he gets into the seat next to the driver, the person is not allowing himself to be driven before the driver turns on the ignition switch (*Diggin*).

So answer D is almost correct. However, it is essential that a conveyance be moved in order for it to be taken, however small that movement may be, and this is the same even though the accused is only allowing himself to be carried. Answer D is therefore incorrect.

Question 22

Answer C — This offence was created to try to prevent the increasing criminal activity involving mobile handsets. The offence is committed where the unique identifier is either changed or interfered with, and is not reliant on a future sale of the phone; answers B and D are therefore incorrect. There is, however, a statutory defence, exclusive to manufacturers or those with written consent of the manufacturers; answer A is therefore incorrect.

Question 23

Answer **D** — On a charge of obtaining property by deception contrary to the Theft Act 1968, s. 15(1), the prosecution must prove that the accused acted dishonestly and with the intention of permanently depriving another of the property. As to intention permanently to deprive, the whole of the definition of this concept in the Theft Act 1968, s. 6, is applicable to s. 15 by virtue of s. 15(3). In this question, the accused does not have such intention; answer A is therefore incorrect.

The Theft Act 1978, s. 1(2), defines 'services' in terms of benefits (which would include accommodation, travel, education, medical care, etc.), but excludes benefits which are provided gratuitously. In *R v Halai* [1983] Crim LR 624, the Court of Appeal held that a building society had not provided services merely by allowing the accused to open a savings account because building societies do not charge any fees for such accounts. The position would be different if the accused practices his deception in order to open a current account with a bank which charges for services provided to such accounts (*R* v *Shortland* [1995] Crim LR 893). It was also held in *Halai* that a mortgage advance falls outside the definition of 'services'. This ruling was widely criticised (and seems down right daft) but has been captured by the Theft Act 1978, s. 1(3), which was inserted by the Theft (Amendment) Act 1996, s. 4. This puts the situation of obtaining a loan by deception squarely within the offence of obtaining services; answers B and C are therefore incorrect.

11 | Criminal Damage

STUDY PREPARATION

The definition of criminal damage needs attention in the first instance, and you will have to know the various components, such as lawful excuse, protection, recklessness, damage, property and belonging to another. In addition to these statutory issues there are many decided cases on each of these points.

It is important to learn the basic definition, before turning to the aggravated offences. Each one of these is similar to the other, with the defendant's intent being of key significance.

It is also worth paying attention to contamination of goods. Although the offences associated with the definition are reasonably long and complicated, this is an area that may receive considerable further attention in the current climate of terrorist threats.

This is the penultimate chapter for you to tackle — you're almost there . . .

QUESTIONS

Question 1

PETERS lived in the countryside and was having trouble with a fox, which had attacked her cat. One day she managed to corner the fox in her neighbour's field, but it escaped into a hole. PETERS set fire to the grass surrounding the hole, but unfortunately, the fire spread to her neighbour's shed. When the fire was eventually extinguished, they found that the fox had been killed, as well as two of the farmer's chickens and some wild geese that he had tamed some time before.

> Given that PETERS may be guilty of reckless criminal damage to property (the shed), would she also be guilty of criminal damage to any of the animals?

A Yes, to the chickens only.
B Yes, to the chickens and the geese.
C No, as animals are not property.
D Yes, to all three animals.

Question 2

POWERS and WARNE were in the centre of their local town. It had been snowing and they decided to have a snowball fight. POWERS made a snowball, and threw it at WARNE, who ducked. The snowball smashed through a nearby shop window. POWERS was arrested, but says in his interview that he had not realised that any damage would be caused.

What must the arresting officers prove in order to show that he had been reckless?

A That the risk of damage to the window was obvious and POWERS should have seen that risk.
B That the risk of damage to the window would have been obvious to a reasonably intelligent person and that POWERS ignored that risk.
C That the risk of damage to the window would have been obvious to POWERS if he had stopped to think about it.
D That the risk of damage to some property was obvious and a reasonable person would have seen the risk.

Question 3

SINGH worked in a car park. While at work on a very hot day, he was told about a dog that was locked in one of the cars, with the windows closed. SINGH went to the car and saw the dog lying on the back seat. He thought that the dog was suffering and, believing that the owner would have consented, he smashed the window. As he was doing this, the owner of the car, MORGAN, returned. It appeared that the dog had not been there long, and it was asleep. MORGAN accused SINGH of causing criminal damage.

In relation to the defence under s. 5(2)(a) of the Criminal Damage Act 1971 (belief that he had consent to the damage to the property in question) only, which of the following statements is correct?

A SINGH could claim this defence, if he could show that a reasonable person would have consented to the damage.
B SINGH could claim this defence if he believed that MORGAN would have consented, had she known the circumstances.

C SINGH could *not* claim this defence as he was reckless in these circumstances.
D SINGH could *not* claim this defence as MORGAN, knowing the circumstances, would not have consented.

Question 4

When proving an offence under s. 1(2) of the Criminal Damage Act 1971 (aggravated criminal damage), what *mens rea* must be shown?
A That the person intended to cause criminal damage and intended to endanger a person's life.
B That the person intended or was reckless as to whether damage would be caused, and intended or was reckless as to whether life would be endangered.
C That the person intended or was reckless as to whether a person's life would be endangered.
D That the person intended to cause criminal damage, and was reckless as to whether a person's life would be endangered.

Question 5

Constable LING saw FRANKIE in a stolen Ford Mondeo in a country lane. The officer pursued the car, but lost sight of it. FRANKIE later abandoned the car next to an occupied house and set fire to it, to remove traces of himself. He did not care whether the house also caught fire or what happened to the occupants of the house. Constable LING later charged FRANKIE with criminal damage to the car, which was valued at £4,000.

In relation to where FRANKIE should be tried for this offence, which of the following statements is correct?
A He may elect to be tried in the Magistrates' Court, because of the value of the damage was less than £5,000.
B He must be tried in the Crown Court, because the value of the damage was more than £2,000.
C He must be tried in the Crown Court regardless of the amount of damage, in these circumstances.
D He can be tried in either the Crown Court or the Magistrates' Court, because the value of the damage was more than £3,000.

Question 6

When considering an offence under s. 2 of the Criminal Damage Act 1971 (threats to destroy or damage property), what must the prosecution prove?

A That the accused intended that the victim would fear that the damage would be carried out immediately.
B That the accused intended to cause damage and intended to induce fear that damage would be carried out.
C That the accused intended that the victim would fear that the damage would be carried out.
D That the victim did in fact fear that the accused would carry out the threat to cause damage.

Question 7

WILKINS and MARTIN are members of an extreme animal rights group. MARTIN applied for a job in a zoo and they planned that if he was successful, he would damage customers' cars by placing sharp tacks under the tyres. WILKINS bought ten packets of tacks at a DIY store the day before MARTIN's interview, intending to give them to him if he got the job.

Has either person committed an offence under s. 3 of the Criminal Damage Act 1971 (having articles with intent to damage property)?

A Only WILKINS; he has control of the articles, intending that MARTIN should use them to cause damage.
B Neither person, as WILKINS does not intend to use the articles himself to cause criminal damage.
C Both people, because of their joint intent that MARTIN should use the articles to cause damage.
D Neither person, as the intent to commit damage is conditional on MARTIN being successful in his interview.

Question 8

THATCHER works in a butcher's shop. As a joke, on 1 April he came in early and sprinkled icing sugar on some meat on display. He then left a note for his boss, claiming to be from an animal rights group, saying they had sprinkled rat poison on the food. Unfortunately, before he was able to stop him, his boss threw the meat away.

Has THATCHER committed an offence contrary to s. 38 of the Public Order Act 1986 (contamination of goods)?

A Yes, because he has caused economic loss to his employer.
B No, because he has not caused public alarm or anxiety.

C No, because he has not actually contaminated any goods.
D No, because he only intended his employer to treat it as a joke.

ANSWERS

Question 1

Answer **B** — Section 10 of the Criminal Damage Act 1971 describes 'property' as:

> ... property of a tangible nature, whether real or personal, including money and —
> (a) including wild creatures which have been tamed or are ordinarily kept in captivity...;

Quite simply, the geese have been tamed and are therefore 'property'. Likewise, the chickens are ordinarily kept in captivity and are therefore 'property'. The fox is not 'property', as it is neither tamed, nor ordinarily kept in captivity. Consequently, answers A, C and D are incorrect.

Question 2

Answer **D** — To prove recklessness in criminal damage, the prosecution must show that a person has done an act, which creates an obvious risk that property will be damaged *and either*, he has not given any thought to the possibility of damage *or* he has seen the risk and has carried on (*Metropolitan Police Commissioner* v *Caldwell* [1982] AC 341).

The risk of damage at the time of the defendant's conduct need only be apparent to a *reasonable person* (which is why answer D is correct and answer A is incorrect).

It is not necessary to show that the risk would have been obvious to the defendant had he or she stopped to think about what he or she was doing (making answer C incorrect); neither need it be shown that the risk would have been obvious to a person of the same age or state of mind as the defendant (*R* v *Coles* [1995] 1 Cr App R 157), which is why answer B is incorrect.

Question 3

Answer **B** — A person shall be treated as having lawful excuse under s. 5(2) of the Criminal Damage Act 1971 if:

(a) if at the time of the act or acts alleged to constitute the offence he believed that the person or persons whom he believed to be entitled to consent to the destruction of or damage to the property in question had so consented, or would have so consented to it if he or they had known of the destruction or damage and its circumstances . . .

Provided a person holds a genuine reasonably held belief that the owner of the property would have consented, had they known the circumstances, they will not be guilty of an offence. (It must be based on the defendant's own belief, not a reasonable person or the owner of the property, making answers A and D incorrect).

Singh is not guilty of recklessness he intended to break the window (making C incorrect).

Question 4

Answer **B** — A person is guilty of an offence under s. 1(2) of the Criminal Damage Act 1971, if they damage/destroy property intending *or* reckless as to whether damage is caused to their own property, or another's, *and* they intend *or* are reckless as to whether a person's life is endangered.

Either the elements of intent *or* recklessness must be proved, in relation to both the damage and the endangerment to life for this offence to be made out. All four answers are fairly similar, but only answer B contains all the elements required to prove the offence. Consequently, answers A, C and D are incorrect.

Question 5

Answer **C** — A person who is guilty of an offence under section 1(3) of the Criminal Damage Act 1971, (arson or criminal damage by fire) where life is endangered, **must** be tried in the Crown Court (on indictment). This is because of the aggravated nature of the offence. (This includes recklessness as to whether life is endangered.)

If a person is charged with simple criminal damage, the offence is normally triable either way. However, if the value of the damage caused is more than £5,000, the case must be tried in the Crown Court. Answers A, B and D are incorrect.

Question 6

Answer **C** — This is an offence of intention; that is, the key element is the *defendant's intention* that the person receiving the threat fears it would be carried out.

The s. 2 offence under the Criminal Damage Act 1971, which originates from the need to tackle protection racketeers, is very straightforward: there is no need to show that the other person actually feared or even believed that the threat would be carried out (making answer D incorrect).

Also, there is no need to show that the defendant intended to carry out the threat; nor does it matter whether the threat was even capable of being carried out (which is why answer B is incorrect).

Answers A and C are similar; however, C is correct because there is no requirement to show that the accused intended to cause fear of *immediate* damage.

Question 7

Answer **A** — Section 3 of the Criminal Damage Act 1971 states:

> A person who has anything in his custody or under his control, intending without lawful excuse to use it or cause or permit another to use it—
> (a) to destroy or damage any property belonging to some other person; or
> (b) to destroy or damage his own or the user's property in a way which he knows is likely to endanger the life of some other person; shall be guilty of an offence.

Answer B is incorrect, as a person may have control of articles which they intend to permit another to use. Answer C is incorrect, as Martin did not have the articles in his custody or control at any time.

Answer D is incorrect because a conditional intention to use an article if given circumstances arise will amount to an offence (*R v Buckingham* (1976) 63 Cr App R 159).

Question 8

Answer **D** — Under s. 38 of the Public Order Act 1986, it is necessary to prove that a person contaminated or interfered with goods, or made it appear that goods have been contaminated or interfered with, or threatened or claimed to have done so.

However, the person must have done so *with the intention* of causing public alarm or anxiety, or of causing injury to members of the public consuming or using the goods, or of causing economic loss to any person by reason of the goods being shunned by members of the public, or of causing economic loss to any person by reason of steps taken to avoid such alarm or anxiety, injury or loss.

Therefore, even though THATCHER in the circumstances may have contaminated goods, and even caused economic loss, he did not do so with the required intention; and cannot be guilty of this offence. (Answer A is therefore incorrect.)

Had THATCHER been proved to have had the required intent, answers B and C would still be incorrect, because there is no need to prove a person actually caused public alarm/anxiety, and the offence may be committed without actually contaminating goods.

12 Offences Against the Administration of Justice and Public Interest

> **STUDY PREPARATION**
>
> This chapter tests your knowledge of those offences which exist to deter people from interfering with the proper course of justice. These offences include perjury and offences relating to false statements all of which are viewed very seriously by our courts. The Common Law offence of perverting the course of justice is included, as are the statutory offences of intimidating witnesses and jurors. Particular crimes relating to those who assist offenders by protecting or hiding them are tested, as are those relating to wasting police time — an area that may also come into greater use as pressures on police resources intensify. Finally, contempt of court and corruption bring the chapter, the book and your studies to an end.
>
> Well done!

QUESTIONS

Question 1

DAVIDSON is giving evidence in court in his own defence. He is not religious and has taken the affirmation instead of swearing on the Bible. The evidence he gives is that he was not at the scene of the offence, stating he was elsewhere. This is in fact untrue and DAVIDSON knows it.

Has DAVIDSON committed perjury?

A No, perjury cannot be committed by a defendant.
B No, perjury can only be committed by a 'sworn' witness.

C Yes, provided it is shown he intended to mislead the court.
D Yes, he has given false testimony and knows it to be false.

Question 2

BOWDITCH has committed an offence which, though not an 'arrestable' offence as per s. 24 of the Police and Criminal Evidence Act, nevertheless carries a statutory power of arrest. Constable SOUTHALL is making enquiries into the whereabouts of BOWDITCH and goes to BOWDITCH's sister's house to see if he is there. BOWDITCH is in fact in the house, and his sister knows he is. BOWDITCH has told her that he committed the offence. Constable SOUTHALL asks the sister if she has seen BOWDITCH. She says she hasn't and that he has gone to his cousin's home in Manchester. Having no reason to disbelieve her, the officer leaves intending to pursue the matter with Greater Manchester Police.

Which of the following statements is true?
A The sister has committed an offence of assisting an offender.
B The sister has committed an offence of harbouring an offender.
C The sister has not committed an offence of assisting an offender.
D The sister has committed no offence.

Question 3

BOWDEN is the local authority building works manager. Aware that his girlfriend has just moved into a new, rather dilapidated house, BOWDEN arranges for a team of workers from the council to go to her house and do some work. They use materials that were meant for council premises and they do the work in council time.

Considering corruption offences, which, if any, offence has BOWDEN committed?
A Common law corruption.
B Public bodies corruption.
C Corruption of agents.
D He has not committed any offence of corruption.

Question 4

SUTTON makes a mobile telephone call to his neighbour stating that a child has just fallen into the river and been swept downstream. His neighbour calls the police and a search commences. Several officers are involved, and the force air support unit are called in to assist. Later SUTTON admits he made the incident up as he had received a speeding ticket last week. In total 25 police hours were wasted and the cost came to £21,000.

Which of the following statements is true?
A SUTTON is guilty of wasting police time as the limit of 21 hours has been passed.
B SUTTON is guilty of wasting police time as he falsely raised fears for the safety of a person.
C SUTTON is not guilty of wasting police time as he did not contact the police himself.
D SUTTON is not guilty of wasting police time as the cost did not exceed £25,000.

Question 5

KANG is originally from Pakistan, but is now a British citizen. His brother (who is not a British citizen) wishes to come to Britain on a permanent basis, but has falsely filled out an entry application stating he is coming on holiday. KANG has signed this form to say that his brother will stay with him on holiday for two weeks. KANG knows this to be false.

Who if either commits an offence contrary to s. 24A of the Immigration Act 1971?
A KANG only, as a British citizen.
B Both KANG and his brother.
C His brother only, as he is not a British citizen.
D Neither, this offence only applies to applications for citizenship.

Question 6

MULLINS has been sold laminate flooring, which is defective and has issued a county court claim against ACME Co. Ltd, who supplied the goods. CROCKETT is an expert laminate floor fitter and intends to give evidence on MULLIN's behalf at court. In order to prevent this, ACME's managing director have written a letter to CROCKETT warning him that he will lose business if he gives evidence against the company.

Does this letter amount to intimidation of a witness?
A Yes, provided there was intention to intimidate CROCKETT.
B Yes, provided the company were reckless as to whether CROCKETT would be intimidated.
C No, as the threat was not made in person.
D No, intimidating witnesses only applies to criminal courts cases, not county courts.

Question 7

LANEY is an accredited Police Community Support Officer (PCSO) and is dealing with ARMSTRONG for a fixed penalty offence and requires ARMSTRONG to provide his name and address. ARMSTRONG refuses and LANEY exercises his power of detention as provided by Schedule 4 of the Police Reform Act 2002. ARMSTRONG is less than impressed at this and pushes the PCSO over and makes good his escape.

Consider the offence at Common Law of Escaping
A ARMSTRONG has committed this offence, and is arrestable.
B ARMSTRONG has committed this offence; however, there is no power of arrest.
C ARMSTRONG has not committed this offence, as it relates to escaping from prisons etc.
D ARMSTRONG has not committed this offence, and it relates to lawful custody, i.e. by a police officer.

ANSWERS

Question 1

Answer **D** — Section 1(1) of the Perjury Act 1911 states:

> If any person lawfully sworn as a witness or as an interpreter in a judicial proceeding wilfully makes a statement material in that proceeding, which he knows to be false or does not believe to be true, he shall be guilty of perjury . . .

Any person includes the defendant and therefore answer A is incorrect. There is no requirement to show intention to mislead the court; simply making the statement deliberately is enough and therefore answer C is incorrect. It is possible for a witness or interpreter to make a solemn affirmation in place of the oath, whether or not the taking of an oath would be contrary to his or her religious beliefs, and s. 15(2) of the Perjury Act 1911 provides that references therein to 'oaths' and 'swearing' embrace affirmations. The affirming witness is therefore equally subject to the Perjury Act 1911 and answer B is also incorrect.

Question 2

Answer **C** — The offence of assisting offenders applies only where an arrestable offence (as per s. 24 of the Police and Criminal Evidence Act) has been committed and therefore answer A is incorrect. Harbouring offenders applies to people who have escaped from a prison or other institutions and therefore answer B is incorrect. The sister has almost certainly committed an offence of perverting the course of public justice and arguably wasting police time. Therefore, contrary to s. 5(2) of the Criminal Law Act 1967, answer D is incorrect.

Question 3

Answer A — Common law corruption is described in *R v Bembridge* (1783) 3 Doug 327: '[a] man accepting an office of trust concerning the public is answerable criminally to the King for misbehaviour in his office . . . by whomever and in whatever way the officer is appointed'. In *R v Bowden* [1996] 1 WLR 98, the Court of Appeal held that a local authority manager, who improperly arranged for his men to carry out work at his girlfriend's house, was guilty of the offence of common law corruption. Public bodies corruption is defined in the Public Bodies Corrupt Practices Act 1889 as 'every person who shall by himself or by or in conjunction with any other person, corruptly solicit or receive, or agree to receive, for himself, or for any other person, any gift, loan, fee, reward, or advantage', which is not the case here so answer B is incorrect. Corruption of agents is described in the Prevention of Corruption Act 1906 as 'if any agent corruptly accepts or obtains, or agrees to accept or attempts to obtain, from any person, for himself or for any other person, any gift or consideration as an inducement or reward', which again is not the case here, so answer C is incorrect. As an offence has been committed, answer D is incorrect.

Question 4

Answer B — The definition of this offence (Criminal Law Act 1967, s. 5(2)) includes the phrase 'making to any person a false report' and therefore answer C is incorrect. Contrary to popular belief there is no time limit for this offence, and answer A is also incorrect. Likewise, there is no monetary value placed on this offence and therefore answer D is incorrect.

Question 5

Answer C — Section 24A of the Immigration Act 1971 is aimed at the actions of non-British citizens only, so as a British citizen, KANG can never commit this offence (answers A and B are incorrect). It applies to any application to obtain or seek to obtain leave to enter the UK in any circumstances, including holidays and therefore answer D is incorrect. Kang's brother commits the offence as he uses means which include deception to achieve his leave to enter. Kang would, however, still commit offences contrary to the interests of justice.

Question 6

Answer A — Section 39 of the Criminal Justice and Police Act 2001 extended the offences of intimidation of witnesses offences outlined in s. 51 of the Criminal Justice and Public Order Act 1994 to proceedings in civil cases. The 1994 Act applies to the investigation or trial of those in criminal proceedings. Answer D is therefore incorrect. The new offence is very similar to the 1994 Act offence and is an offence of specific intent, so recklessness will not suffice (answer B is therefore incorrect). The offence includes doing any act provided it was with the intention of intimidating a witness and provided the defendant knew the person might be a witness. This would include writing letters, making phone calls, etc., and is not limited to personal threats (answer C is also incorrect).

Question 7

Answer A — This offence applies to persons in lawful custody, anywhere. It is not restricted to custody units, prison, etc. Answer C is therefore incorrect. Whether a person is 'in custody' or not is a question of fact and the word 'custody' is to be given its ordinary meaning (*E* v *DPP* [2002] EWHC 433). This could be shown by providing evidence that the person's liberty was restricted (as it is in the question), and that it was lawful (Sch. 4 of the 2002 act provides this). This custody is not the restricted to sworn police officers; therefore, answer D is incorrect and would include PCSOs Investigating Officers or Escort Officers who are given powers by the 2002 Act. The offence of escaping is an indictable offence and is arrestable; therefore, answer B is incorrect.